Love Can
Open Prison Doors

By
Starr Daily

Author of "Release"

TO DAD TRUEBLOOD, A WISE OLD LIFER, AND A TRUE FRIEND, TO YOU I DEDICATE THIS HUMBLE EFFORT, AND REMEMBER YOU ALWAYS AS EVERY GRATEFUL PUPIL SHOULD REMEMBER HIS KIND AND PATIENT MASTER

Stone walls do not a prison make,
Nor iron bars a cage;
He is not free who beats his wings
In bitterness and rage:
That man alone is free who loves
Creative virtue's way,
But dares to reach a hand to those
In the clutches of decay.

—Paraphrase of Lovelace

CONTENTS

FOREWORD

During one of his radio broadcasts, "The Love Way," Dr. Victor Paul Wierwille shared:

I have sometimes wondered what would happen if a man really dared to go all the way out to the limit of love. ...There are very few people who ever believe in love. They believe in force, they believe in intrigue, they believe in self and sense-knowledge judgments and arguments, but do they believe in love?

Dr. Wierwille had met one of those rare individuals who did believe in the unlimited power of the love of God. He was an inspiring Christian speaker and author, then known as Starr Daily. On January 18, 1952, Starr was the first guest speaker at Dr. Wierwille's, "The Spiritual 40 Club." He was also a regular teacher at Glenn Clark's popular Camps Farthest Out. This shining example of Christ's love touched and changed the lives of innumerable people through his powerful, personal testimony of how the force of love can release anyone from physical, mental and spiritual bondage. The message struck people even more powerfully when they discovered their speaker's past.

In the early 1900s, Starr Daily was a hardened criminal, the kind of man who seemed destined to spend his life behind bars. Filled with hate from the tender age of eight years old, Starr had already run afoul of the law repeatedly by the time he reached adolescence. Uncaring and calloused to the suffering of others, Daily admits that he "...harmed thousands, many very brutally." Glenn Clark writes of Starr Daily in his book, *From Crime To Christ*:

> For twenty-five years, in fact, he hated all mankind. Like the outcast Ishmael, his hand was against every man, and every man's hand was against him. When he was sixteen years old he met an extraordinary character. A man who was the advance agent of a group of safe breakers took him under his wing much as old Fagin took Oliver Twist and put him through special training in crime. ... In time he became a captain of a team which was so skillful in its operations that it baffled all the skill of the Pinkertons to catch them or to hold them when caught. Had Starr kept away from liquor he would never have been caught. Then followed a period when, for fourteen years, he was a member of chain gangs or confined in penitentiaries.

America's penal system in the early 20th century certainly violated the constitutional prohibition against "cruel and unusual punishment." In fact, most of today's world would deem it barbaric, disregarding basic human rights in many respects. Flogging, torture, starvation, brutally hard labor, and prolonged periods of solitary confinement were common practice in the prisons of that era, and a common experience for Starr Daily. He was beaten with rubber hoses and blackjacks, tortured with lighted cigars, hung by handcuffs from a hot steam pipe, and fed only bread and water in solitary confinement for fifteen days at a stretch. Determined to never allow his sadistic jailers to break him, he survived through the force of this hatred for them. Daily was in every way a dangerous, caged animal, controlled by fear and hate, and living life by the dictates of the "prison mentality." He scoffed at the "do-gooders" who tried to reform him while he worked to manipulate them to his advantage; he struck out at anyone he perceived as a threat. And after being turned down repeatedly for parole, he resigned himself to the seemingly inevitable fate of spending his life in chains.

Everyone, including Starr himself, believed that he was beyond rehabilitation and without hope in this world. When his father died, he perhaps lost the last person on earth who loved him; a father who prayed and did everything that he could to help his son. The world may have given up on Starr Daily, and Starr may have given up on himself. Yet, while no person on earth found him worth saving, in a phenomenal manner, Starr met his Savior, the Lord Jesus Christ.

Then, like the poet once said, he was "touched by the Master's hand." Where HATE had once been the driving force of his life, now LOVE ruled. The love of God changed Starr Daily; and as he learned to walk in that love, he changed his circumstances, the people around him, the prison institution, and the course of his life.

In many respects, today's world is a different place than the world Starr wrote about. Prison reform has brought about many changes to how prisoners are treated; some of the credit for that, in fact, goes to Starr Daily. Times have changed. The vernacular of the early 20th century that Starr spoke occasionally sticks out like the lapels on a Jazz Age suit. But the truth that he speaks about transcends the boundaries of time and location.

Love Can Open Prison Doors does more than tell the story of how one man was changed by God's love. It opens the eyes of the reader to the limitless possibilities of what love can do. If love could open the prison doors of steel, the shackles of fear, the captivity of hate, and the torture chamber of hopelessness that held a wretched convict like Starr Daily; then it can break whatever chains may hold you. Considering how Starr Daily applied the force of love to overcome the most difficult situations one might imagine challenges the Christian believer to release the power of love in their own lives to liberate all held captive.

CHAPTER 1
The Last Experiment

E xcept for idiocy and other conditions of mental invalidism, personal failure is indefensible. The failure is his own indictment and conviction.

During the last two years I have interviewed more than three hundred men and women who have openly admitted they were abject failures in life. In each case I have asked, "Why?" And in every instance the answer has been in the character of an alibi. But in no case has the failure laid the blame for defeat at his or her own door.

In my own experience and in the cases of all others I have found this to be an inescapable truth: that when a man offers an excuse, an alibi for himself, or in any way lays the blame for his weakness, conditions, or failures on some one or some thing outside himself, he is invariably wrong, and in nine cases out of ten he is a weakling and a coward who is roundly condemned by his own spirit.

His alibis may and generally do enlist the sympathy of those upon whom they are practiced. But if he is a normal human being, there is one person who will not accept his offering, and that is the person who is his real self. Mild of manner, easy-going, and infinitely patient, this real person, who dwells silently within him, listens to his excuses and then whispers softly, "You must tell it to your friend George: but not to me."

If you insist, this quiet man within will begin to

shame you with a long string of apt comparisons. He will point out those who have less advantage and native ability, but who are successful. He will take you into the bedrooms of the ill and incapacitated and let you observe courage at work in the service of humanity. He will present you with a long list of names in the huge book of political, industrial, artistic, cultural, civic, religious, and scientific life. Then he will tell you how many of these were practically illiterate, inarticulate, friendless, without direction, influence, or prestige but took advantage of opportunities that have swirled unnoticed about you all your life.

This inner man once spoke to a friend through Thomas Edison. The great inventor and his friend were walking along a city street. The friend wanted to know if it were not very difficult to succeed in this high-speed world of terrific competition. Mr. Edison's eyes directed the gaze of his friend to a ragged, prematurely old man on whose bent shoulders lay a large sack of junk. Then he answered: "Yes; but it is more difficult to fail."

On a day in the spring of 1930 I sat in the cell of a fellow convict. As I had done, he had wasted the best years of his life behind prison bars. He was telling me that he was sick and tired of prison bells, profitless labor, and convict hash. But at forty it was too late to think of turning "Honest John."

I inquired into his particular brand of reasons for failure, because all criminals are failures, whether they be big protected ones who never see prison, or little unprotected ones who rarely see anything else. He had figured it all out and possessed an alibi as iron-clad as the cell door behind which we sat. He could trace it all back to an unhappy instance in his childhood when a too stern father flailed the hide off him because he wanted to see what made the wheels go around in the family clock. Had his unimaginative dad been more appreciative of the genius behind his destructive curiosity, he might now be a mechanical engineer instead of a weary slave in the prison rock quarry.

"I'm dressing out next month," I told him. "And I'm never coming back."

"Whatta ya think you're gonna do?" he asked, giving me a wise smile.

"I learned the tricks of making dishonest money," was my reply, "and to the degree I succeeded I failed. Now I'm going to learn the art of earning an honest living. Isn't that good logic?"

He assured me that eighty per cent of the convicts were two, three, and four-time losers, and that every one of them had made that same remark a thousand times. "But it don't mean anything," he added. "It's just like the resolution a drunk makes on the morning after. He's never gonna take another drink as long as he lives. But in a couple o' hours he's all lit up again, an' everything looks Jake."

I insisted that mine was not an idle New Year's resolution.

"But what can you do? You don't know how to work. When you go out you'll meet twenty million Honest Johns who do know how, and who know all the ropes about getting jobs. They'll be your competitors in the labor market. They're skilled workers; got good names an' reputations. They can face employers with the best. But what have you to offer? Just a life of crime. A penitentiary pallor and a lock-step hitch in your gait. A fat chance you'll have. At best I give you six months to try this bug-house notion. Just long enough for the soup-line to stare you in the face. Then you'll wake up with a bang and blast open the first safe you come across."

He did not understand that I had already wakened with a bang while lying half dead in solitary confinement. There in a moment's time the folly of crime and the stupidity of hatred appeared clear cut in my consciousness, and I got an authentic glimpse of the greatest power in all the world, the power of love, which, when lived with any measure of proficiency, could see you through any emergency, dissolve your toughest problems, cause you to live serenely, triumphantly, and successfully at any time and in any place; that *with love on your side as a philosophy of life every obstacle and opposition could be discerned in its true light, as an opportunity to call forth your power.*

This was a magnificent vision, although I did have to get it through blind suffering. It has sustained me in all the hard hours since I left the prison, and has turned every difficulty into a glorious challenge and blessing.

After I had caught it, my powers of recollection were stimulated, and I wondered how I could have been so blind as not to see that love and not hate was the real power in this world.

Instantly I began to recall events in my past when the truth of love's power had been made so plain that only a midnight soul could have failed to recognize it. Now, looking back, I could see how the power of love had performed strange things in my life.

I recalled a time when I was being held in jail on suspicion of burglary. For two days and nights I had been subjected to "third degree" police methods in an effort to torture a confession out of me. My head had been beaten with a rubber hose until it resembled a huge stone bruise, swollen beyond human shape, my face black from the congealed blood beneath the surface. Lighted cigars had been pressed against my flesh. I had hung for three hours with my wrists handcuffed over a hot steam pipe. My arms had been twisted behind me and my elbows beaten with black-jacks until the bones felt crunchy. Heavy heels had ground my bare feet against a concrete floor. On the third night of this I was about at the end of my endurance.

Again I was dragged into the torture room and sat down within the semi-circle of twelve big detectives. My previous sustaining energy of hate and anger had dwindled into a dull sense of indifference. I was alarmed at this new state of affairs. For I had learned that pain could easily be assimilated if sufficient hatred could be thrown against it. I did not want to weaken. Death was preferable. But could I stand the pain without the sustaining force of hate?

"You'd better open up and come clean," the Chief informed me. "If you don't you're gonna get the works. Y'understand?"

I continued to sit in silence, expecting the worst, and wondering if I would be able to take it.

"All right, boys," said the Chief. "Get busy. Let the rat have it."

It was the show down. Unless I broke, my life was not worth a dime. I knew this as two of the detectives stepped towards me. Then a strange thing took place in my consciousness. All hate and anger were gone. The vague sense of indifference vanished. And in an unbidden instant there welled up within me an overwhelming compassion for these men, for their pathetic ignorance, their undeveloped souls, for the pitiful condition of their minds and hearts. And as this strange sentiment reached a high peak of intensity within me the Chief spoke, and what he said constituted a minor miracle.

"Don't hit him again," he barked out. "Take him back."

I was returned to my cell, and for the remainder of the night I was under the care of a doctor. The next morning I was transferred to a private hospital, where I lived for three weeks. Every day a number of women came to see me, bringing flowers and other gifts. It was all quite mystifying, and the nurses' guarded explanations did not clarify the mystery. These women were the wives of city detectives. I could not figure the thing out. I was only a friendless, unprotected criminal. They had no reason to placate me with gifts and attention because they feared what I might reveal. I was told not to worry about anything, that all bills would be paid. Nor was I returned to the jail on being discharged from the hospital. Instead I was given an envelope and told that I was free to go. In the envelope was no word of explanation. Only five crisp, ten-dollar bills.

It was not until twenty years later, twenty years filled with crime and punishment, that I was able to see through this mystery, and to know the power, because of which my life had been spared and this odd consideration shown me.

On another occasion when I was on the dealer's side of the table, I was an unseeing witness to this transmuting power of love in action. I was robbing the safe in the home of a priest. He surprised me in the act. From a stairway above me I heard his unexpected voice: "What are you doing there, my child?"

I wheeled, my flashlight and gun on him. He was

in a night robe and unarmed. "Stand where you are," I commanded sharply. "I've got you covered."

"I mean you no harm." His voice had a rare accent of kindliness and honor in it. Slowly he began descending the steps.

"Stop, or I'll drop you!" I commanded him. With superb assurance he came on, reached the bottom, and walked leisurely over to a light switch and pressed the button. Turning to me, then, he said: "Put your gun down, my child. I only want to talk with you a little while."

Logically, of course, from my point of view, I was in a close place with the odds in my favour. It was not sound criminal judgment for me to accede to his request. The correct procedure under the circumstances would have been to tie him and gag him, then to proceed with the business at hand.

What a singular thing for me to do! I obeyed him and sat in the chair he pointed out. I say singular, because it was so illogical, unreasonable from the viewpoint of a confirmed crimester—and because, also, I listened to him while he talked to me about God in a most singular way—a way in which there seemed to be nothing offensive to my God-hating mind. God might have been my own father, or an elder brother, or a very close friend, anything but the fierce-eyed black-bearded monster of wrath, anger, and fire I had heard so much about.

At two o'clock in the morning I accepted this priest's invitation, went with him into the kitchen, and joined him in a cold bite. I left his home without taking his money. He shook my hand and blessed me. I had no fear that when I was out of sight he would exercise what the world calls duty and call the police. To this day I am sure he never mentioned my nocturnal visit.

What was this strange power he possessed over me? He did this because his love was genuine, not the romantic, sentimental emotion that men call love; but that deep sense of compassionate being which was so eloquently expressed by the Master when He said "Neither do I condemn thee." Nothing less than love could have caused me to act in a manner diametrically opposite to my habitual character as a criminal.

You see, I am introducing you to my theme. I am telling you about *a power that resides in the hearts of men, which is a power greater than any power ever to be discovered in the realm of natural science.* It is a power possessed by all, but recognized by few. It is the most dynamic and readily accessible power in the universe of men. Every man can contain and express this power. It is practical. And because it is accessible to every man and because it is practical, I am perfectly safe in making again the boldest statement ever made by another human being: that, except by idiocy and other conditions of mental invalidism, failure is indefensible.

Occasionally when a man has suffered enough he will accept this power and use it. Sometimes his suffering is so great that the sheer intensity of his need will awaken him to this power which is closer to him than breath, and will heal him instantly. I call love the "last experiment," because though it is the closest and most fundamental thing in a person's life, it is the last thing he will turn to for help when he is in distress.

In talking to you about love I shall not get mushy and sentimental. For love is everything that sentimentalism is not. Love is power, while sentimentalism is the misuse of power. In its practical application love is as precise and scientific as mathematics. Without it there could be no universe, no cell organization of any kind. Because love is the only integrating power in existence. It is all that can establish order out of chaos or maintain order in chaos. Whenever it is recognized by man he likewise recognizes harmony. Love is never a disintegrating force. Science deals with disintegrating natural forces; but wisdom deals with the power of love. Natural forces lead to change: love to permanence. Love simplifies life. All that is less than pure love complicates it. Love is endurable, eternal. It is the one ultimate expression which can combine and sustain all principles of the natural and spiritual worlds. Its application releases the soul of man from the bondage of limitation. Love is God in action. And the process of becoming the doctrine of love is to grow into oneness with God.

The beautiful thing about the doctrine of love is that it casts out all fear, all striving and struggling. You merely act and express the virtues and qualities of love, and all that is needed to sustain you in happiness and harmony are inevitable consequences of your action. You are attached to nothing except the action of love. You desire no results; but possess perfect assurance that the correct results necessary to your life at a given time will be supplied. *The sense of impending insecurity is unknown to him who lives the doctrine of love.*

With the light of love to guide us the idea of seeking God fades on the film of our consciousness, and we know, then, that this idea, long held and fostered by men, is as false as the beard of Hercules. It is God who is doing the seeking. It is God who stands at our door and knocks. When we consciously and deliberately set out to seek God, we are simply being annoyed by God's seeking us. His incessant pounding on our door gets on our nerves, we try to escape from the friction and irritation of it, and we call this "seeking God." We go to church, or the lecture hall, or drop a coin in the hand of a beggar, or we join a charitable organization. And the more we seek the farther we drift from the real consciousness of God's presence, for we stifle His voice and dull the sound of His knocking. God is the Supreme Shepherd, and it must forever be the logical procedure for the shepherd to seek his lost sheep, and not for the lost sheep to seek him. When we are lost in the woods our sense of direction is gone and we move about in fruitless circles. It is only when we cease seeking our way and sit down and get quiet that we regain our poise and balance sufficiently for intuition to lead us out of our dilemma.

Our job here is to learn to love. It is the only obligation man has in the world. There is no other religion. And it is all the salvation possible. Any service rendered in an effort to placate God is futile. If you think you can serve God while at the same time you have in your mind you are serving God, then you are separating yourself from God. Service to God is present only when the thought of serving Him is absent. When you love the service and think not of rewards or results, or that you are doing it for God in return for His gifts, God will then draw nigh unto you.

The lover always question the correctness in any ethical or moral or philosophical statement that has become platitudinous and hence meaningless. Consequently when he hears the statement "Serve God," he begins to analyze the correctness of the statement. And he discovers it to be a meaningless platitude in its current sense. For he knows that you can perform your charities, your prayers, and your abnegations until doomsday without ever becoming aware of God's presence. But if you really love God, and really serve because you love to serve, and you really pray because you love to pray, then the statement, "Serve God," is not a platitude. It has meaning and salvation in it. And it is rewarded with the gift of God's grace. The statements of Jesus have never degenerated into the category of moral platitudes, because they are firmly rooted in the doctrine of love.

Now this being a very important point, as my book will increasingly endeavor to show, let us dwell just a little longer on the subject. In God service and love are one and the same thing. If we learn to love in the true sense we cannot help serving God. But if, by our wills and misconceptions, we force ourselves to serve with the mistaken notion we are serving God, or if in our service the motivating quality of love is absent, then service and love are separated, and our service is questionable; indeed, it is false and spurious. We must, therefore, learn to love first, and having learned to love, all else is added as a natural consequence.

We begin with the tremendous truth that the only world duty and spiritual obligation we have is to become love, that is, to learn to love and mean it.

Hence if this is our only obligation we begin by learning to love. We learn to love by first practicing love. The more we practice the more we become conditioned to the vibration of love. And in time, if we persist, we actually become a true lover of God and the creatures and creations of God. When this time comes we can serve God, and inevitably will serve Him, and our service will be genuine.

To illustrate this point an example may be employed. Suppose you have a very dear friend. You do something to hurt or offend him. Thereafter something stands between you and your friend. It is an invisible and nameless barrier, which you want to remove. In seeking to remove it you try various ways to serve him. You bring him gifts, or you seek to make influential contacts advantageous to him. In other words, you seek to heal the world in his heart by means of compromise and placation. But the barrier remains. All you do does not wipe away the disappointment in his eyes.

So long as this disappointment is allowed to remain you are separated from your friend, although you associate with him daily. While it remains you cannot serve him effectively, because the server and the object of service are separated. So long as this is so you cannot know how to serve him.

Finally you weary of your thankless efforts, and you go to your friend in a spirit of humility and contrition, and you apologize for your wrong, and you ask him to forgive and forget. The spirit within him meets the spirit within you. All hurt vanishes from his face, to be replaced by a smile of genuine joy. Your old relationship is instantly re-established. And now you can serve him. You bring him a gift that is a gift of real love and affection. You do things for him because you love to do it, and not because in doing it you desire to win back his friendship.

And so it is with God. When His Spirit has become your spirit, when you have actually known Him by a deep inner experience of knowingness, you are capable of serving Him in works, faith, and prayer. But to pray to God without loving God, or without the capacity to love Him, is to render lip service to an unknown God, and the only possible value in such a prayer must be psychological and not spiritual.

Finally when we have suffered and been defeated

enough we shall turn to the last experiment, we shall turn to love and begin to learn to love by practicing love. As we become love we draw God to us; when we know God we cease all straining and quietly lay our burdens in His lap, knowing that He knows best how to dispose of them. But how do we begin the practice of love. Love is charity in the true sense of that misused word, and charity begins at home. Hence we start the practice of love first in our own homes. It is when we learn to love those nearest to us that we are then able to love our neighbors, the citizens of our community, and finally of the state and nation and the world. And then our love reaches out to embrace all nature. *With this accomplishment the Grand Passion is born full-blown in our hearts and we love God with an affection that is holy.* To love Him is not to seek Him longer; but to accept Him who has long been seeking us.

*   *   *   *   *

Since writing this simple chronicle of love in action behind the bars of a modern penitentiary, I have received several hundred letters from all parts of the world. Some have been inspired by reading the book; a few have been repulsed. Many have had their curiosity aroused. Others have found in it the information necessary to effect salutary changes in their lives: they have regained lost health; have solved their environmental and economic problems. All have asked questions concerning statements which were either implied or lightly touched upon in the context. And these questions are the most important features contained in the letters received.

To ask has value. To decide upon the answer has greater value. To act upon the decision is of supreme importance, whether the decision acted upon be good, bad, or indifferent. It is better to keep busy with blunders and mistakes, trials and errors than it is to sit with folded hands and a heart filled with unexpressed and frustrated wishes.

The questions have called forth this introduction. Almost entirely these pages are concerned with the deliberate and conscious application of the Law of Love to the practical everyday problems of life. My readers have unerringly sensed the power of love as being a power within their capacity to recognize and to use. But they have wanted to know more about what love is, as well as how to use it and what it does when used.

I make no claims of a last-word nature. Love can be defined on familiar levels of consciousness. Beyond that it enters mystery and awaits our arrival in another dimension. The following statements we can comprehend:

We cannot escape love. If in the physical body we ceased to love for an instant we should die. *Hate is nothing more than an intense form of self love.* It is a twisting of God's love, causing it to operate negatively rather than positively, destructively rather than constructively in the direction of our own best interests. Because God loves, we love. Our love does not create that which was before. Before our love, was God's love. It is His love which created our love, and which supports, sustains, and expands it. We are partakers of God's love. We act in the direction of those qualities of being which we conceive to be of God. God's love is always creative. We are creative when we express His love in action. As to what His love creates, through us, is a matter of our own choice. To act in the direction of kindness, faith, discrimination, gratitude, reverence, forgiveness, is to build the qualities of constructive love into our personalities. To act in the direction of hate, doubt, in discrimination, ingratitude, unforgivingness, is to build into our personalities the destructive qualities of love.

As Robert E. Speer has pointed out in his work, *Seeking the Mind of Christ:* "His love is the power of our loving. Herein is love, not that we loved God, but that He loved us, and sent His Son to be the propitiation for our sins. If God so loved us we also ought to love one another. We love because He first loved us. God's love did not begin when we began to love God. We never would have loved either God or our brother had it not been for the love of God. His love, whether we knew it or not, begat all our love. Our love of God. . .is but letting Him love us. Our love is but a faint shadow of His, a shadow that advances and retreats and quivers uncertainly. The great and steadfast love of God is not the child of the shadow. Unchanging, measureless, utterly forgiving, rich with the wealth of His infinite nature, the love of God is beneath and above and about our weak human love, and we can rest upon His love as the great certainty beyond all our impulses."

*   *   *   *   *

We swim in an infinite ocean of love. To become increasingly conscious of our oneness with love, is the mark of exercising intelligent self interest. To this end, we do not labor and strain in our search for love. It is above, beneath, and about us. It is seeking us.

To act is the secret. To exercise the capacities we have for love is to expand our capacities for receiving and expressing love. Seeking love is to attempt to define a love which we have not yet developed the capacity to express. How can we understand the love

of the Supreme Lover, except we approach His love
through the process of practice or of daily becoming?
With only a modicum of His capacity for love, how
can we understand the things He did not do:

> "He might have built a palace at a word,
> Who sometimes had not where to lay His head;
> Time was, and He who nourished crowds with bread
> Would not one meal unto Himself afford;
> Twelve legions girded with angelic sword
> Were at His beck, the scorned and buffeted;
> He healed another's scratch, His own side bled,
> Side, feet and hands with cruel piercings gored,
> Oh, wonderful the wonders left undone!
> And scarce less wonderful than those He wrought;
> Oh, self restraint, passing all human thought,
> To have all power, and be as having none;
> Oh, self-denying love, which felt alone
> For needs of others, never for its own."

This is the great love. We move toward it. In this
high sense, love is all a bestowal, a giving of ourselves
with a discriminatory purpose—that of moving in the
right direction. The very air we breathe is a bestowal
of God's love to us. To become aware of this fact is to
be grateful for the grace which makes breathing
possible, and to become aware of love in the smallest
degree is to partake of more of love's inexhaustible
supply. Our out-breath is a bestowal of love whose
chemical qualities support and sustain the lower forms
in nature. To become consciously aware of this
unselfish process is the important thing for us, for
increasing awareness is the measure of expanding
consciousness, and expanding consciousness is the
increasing capacity for receiving, containing, and
expressing the love which God has bestowed upon us.

This book, therefore, is an indication of a way. It
points out the modus operandi of one man who caught
a glimpse of the love theme in the stillness of a dun-

geon cell. Its keynote is response; its purpose is not definition, but inspiration. To be inspired is to want to act. The book being true, it must inspire, to cause the reader to want to act. How to begin to act and how to continue to act; in a word, how consciously to apply the dynamic power of love to the every day problems confronting the personality life—this is or should be the aim of any book dealing with personal experience of this kind.

One thing is certain, no man or woman can act in the direction of bestowal unseen or unrewarded. Man acts and the Spirit observes.

CHAPTER 2
Love Versus Dungeon Doors

When I say that love can open prison doors I mean that literally. When I say there are doors much stronger than the doors of a punitive prison, I mean that literally also. But when I speak of this love I'm not referring to it in the usual Pollyanna sense, as something to be hazily realized and half heartedly applied.

Love is a dynamic force in the world. It is the most powerful creative force in existence, and it is responsible for nearly everything created by and through man. Love for God, for charity, for service; love for money, for power, for fame—all or any one of these urges will drive men and women to use the creative principle that sends them to the top of their respective desires. But since all human desire is insatiable it is never fully gratified. Creative progress is made in proportion as the driving love medium behind ambition goads the goal-climber into action.

Love for debauchery, for crime, for the gratification of pig-sty appetites send men and women toward the bottom that represents the goal of *their* respective desires. But again since human desire is insatiable, the gratification sought is never found. Creative degradation is advanced in proportion as the love driving media for degradation is used toward its end.

Behind the creation of an infant lies the contacting medium of love. And since that love is human it produces a human being, and thus perpetuates the human race with all its human desires and aspirations, its human follies and mistakes, its trials and errors, its tragedies and humors, its enormous conceits and egotism that cause it to survive through all the elemental cataclysms and plagues to which the earth is heir.

Love for opinion makes saints and scoundrels, martyrs and tyrants out of men. Love for publicity and notoriety makes heroes and dare-devils. *Love for self creates bigotry; for others, tolerance.*

Always love is a medium through which man contacts and applies the creative principle of the universe. And what love is allowed to create through man is up to man himself. His love attitude determines the course taken by creative principle. Inevitably, the creative principle operating on and through man, creates something; something noble or ignoble, constructive or destructive.

The principle in itself is ultimate unity, and is therefore not subject to finite discriminatory limitations. It is beyond time, space, duality, judgment, because in it all things are dissolved into the changeless whole. It has but one purpose, one nature, one reason for being, and that is to create. And create is what it does. There is neither good nor bad connected with its creative purpose. These are human discernments recognized by man and obeyed by creative principle. The principle being infinite and discernment finite on the plane of duality, it follows that man can use creative law only in the ratio of his capacity to receive it, and no more. One may sink as low as his faculties of invention are capable of carrying him; one, may rise as high as his understanding and application will reach.

The foregoing is no attempt to define love, because that cannot be done. All definitions limit and the limitless cannot be limited, pigeon-holed, or labelled. He who would seek to define the indefinable would only curb his capacity for using it. Consequently, what I have said should be taken for what I have intended it to be, a description rather than an exposition.

Also, when you read this, please understand clearly that I am not a reformed convict, because the term reform has lost the whole of its pristine meaning. Its purity has been defiled by many unwholesome connotations; too much Comstockism, commercialism and hypocrisy have been attached to it in recent years, especially, to warrant my associating myself with it in these pages. The term has become the living symbol of suppression and all that is mean and narrow in human conduct and behavior. Rather, I wish to be looked upon here, not as a reformed criminal, but as a fool who has been privileged to shake off a little of his foolishness; at least to the extent of realizing that a fool's paradise isn't all it's cracked up to be.

In every prison they have many unjust rules, the same as every nation has many unjust laws. One of these rules in the prison where I was last confined had to do with what is called, for some strange reason, "the right to trial."

This right was vouchsafed the prisoner charged with violating prison law in what was known as "High Court." This court was in session twice weekly. It consisted of the deputy warden, who was its prosecutor, judge and jury. When you entered in to answer the complaint placed against you by your warder, the deputy would read the charge and then command you to admit your guilt to it. Why all this mockery and waste of time that could have been better employed was, of course, a mystery. Certainly the court was unnecessary since your accuser's word was infallible. If you denied your guilt and thus dared to infer your innocence, your action was equivalent to calling your warder a liar, and this implication was certain to increase the amount of punishment meted out, unless, like Galileo, you were diplomatic enough to change your mind and recant. The theory seemed to be that the aspersion "liar" was a natural characteristic of the prisoner, but that all prison warders were George Washington who couldn't possibly tell a lie.

Naturally, nearly every one recanted sooner or later. Some had to be persuaded by a few weeks in the dungeon on bread and water, it is true. But so far as I know I was the only man haled before the prison court who preferred slow death by starvation rather than life by an admission of guilt. There was no principle involved in my stand. None at all, other than just plain hard-headedness. I was not rebelling against an act of injustice, because I was sufficiently honest to admit that my whole life had been built upon injustice toward others, and that all things being equal I had injustice coming to me. No, I was simply exercising a foolish prerogative to remain obstinate regardless of the pain and physical consequences.

It was in the middle of an exceptionally bitter winter. The torture chamber was damp, foul, and dark. The stone walls were full of frost; the concrete floors were wet and icy. You were put into a cell with nothing but a thin, much-washed shirt and overalls. Your shoes were taken away, but you were allowed to retain your socks. At night the keeper of the dungeon brought you a thin and filthy cotton blanket.

Such is a brief picture of the place I entered to

carry out my own self-inflicted verdict of death. When he put me into the cell the deputy warden said: "When I let you out you'll crawl to me on your knees and whine and beg like a dog. And while you're in here eating bread and water, I'll be living on ham and eggs and sleeping in a good warm bed."

Knowing the man as I did, I had no reason on earth to believe he might suddenly become chicken-hearted and relent. On the other hand, I told him in reply, and I knew I meant it, that his rats would carry me out a chuck at a time before I'd ever whine to him. Obviously, therefore, my fate was sealed as tightly as it could be sealed by two human wills in conflict.

And yet I was finally released from the dungeon weak but alive and an infinitely wiser person. I had done no whining or begging of any kind. In fact, from the day I entered until the day I was released no word passed between the deputy warden and me. He came each day and opened the solid door of my cell, stood there a moment in silence to give me a chance to speak, then he would close the door and pass on to his next victim.

*   *   *   *   *

Although I am engaged here with a few chosen events in my life, and in nowise with an autobiography, it is necessary for me to digress at this point if the reader would be spared the annoyance of numerous digressions later on. Certain things in my life prior to the dungeon experience touched upon, which have a relative importance as bearing upon that experience, must be traced out for a clearer understanding of what might otherwise appear to border on the miraculous or the impossible.

It is the usual thing to suppose that one's dream life is closely associated with and to a great extent influenced by one's conscious life. And this is true to a great extent. No doubt the dream which I shall later describe would seem too far-fetched and contrary were it to stand alone unsupported by conditioning causes.

Since I was a person who for many years followed a criminal career, whose every thought and action during those years had been in violent contrast to all precepts of common decency, it is only reasonable to conclude that my dream life would have revolved pretty much around a similar pattern. Or at least that my dream life could hardly have been expected to revolve around holy and superior things.

But even though the years have a way of blurring the most vivid experiences of childhood, the historic cycle has a peculiar penchant for resurrecting those experiences, both in the conscious and subconscious realms of activity; of duplicating events; of repeating incidents, which in their day were passed over as having no apparent significance.

I wish to say now that as a small child my dreams were frequently woven around the personality of Jesus, although in my home there was no particular stress laid upon religious things, or upon the Saviour's ministry as it was recorded in the Bible. I had no leaning toward church service, and I was not compelled to attend Sunday school. Despite these omissions, nevertheless, my early dream life invariably had to do with things of a holy nature.

Then at twelve years of age I began a series of minor crimes, which soon developed into major ones. At fourteen I was a confirmed criminal with all the bitter, negative philosophy possessed by the toughest of the men who prey. This transition did not affect the intensity of my dream life, but it did greatly affect the quality of my dreams.

My early dreams of Jesus had always been laid in a strange beautiful garden, different from any garden I had ever seen, heard of, or read about. It was a shoe-shaped valley plot surrounded by gently sloping tree and shrub-dotted hills. There were many varieties of flowers growing wild. At one end of the garden a great white grey rock jutted out and from behind it or through it, I could never quite tell which, the Master would emerge and walk toward me, carefully avoiding the flowers as He moved slowly along.

The pattern of these dreams changed promptly with the pattern of my life. The peaceful garden through which the Master strolled under Judean stars and dew-freshened dawns, became a merciless jungle filled with gun-toting enemies, emissaries of the law, all bent upon my capture.

In rapid succession of events, I would envision myself under arrest, of being tried in court and convicted. I would hear the grim verdict read and listen to the terrifying pronouncement of sentence. I could experience all the agony of suspense that stretched between the day of sentence pronounce-ment and the day of its execution. Sometimes I would see myself being escorted to the scaffold or the electric chair behind a dour-faced individual mum-bling gloomy prayers for the safe journey of my sin-tainted soul. Very often I would reach the lethal monster and feel the black cap being drawn over my face, like a fiendish bandage, or the straps being adjusted to my legs. But invariably I would wake in the nick of time, trembling, sweating, exhausted.

I've passed through the hot pits of many tortures, but none to compare to these subconscious hours where deferred judgment assumed all the hideous aspects of actuality.

That they were prophetic dreams I have no doubt. Criminal activities always lead toward the commission of murder and murder toward the executioner. And yet the fear of these sinister prospects was not sufficient to alter the course of my criminal tendencies. In fact, neither fear of punishment nor persuasion, kind treatment or brutal, had any effect on the type of life I preferred to live.

During my many years in prison I was the object of a great deal of well-intentioned kindness, as well as harshness. Different social workers tried to influence my attitude. These good people were called sobsters in the prison vernacular. We used to vie with each other for their gifts and favors, and whatever influence, political, they might bring to bear upon parole-boards in our behalf. But always their advice was an extremely obnoxious service which we assumed to relish, lest we forfeit the opportunity of using our advisers toward other ends.

Sometimes they would come to the prison chapel and make sentimental speeches, exhorting us to put on the raiment of reformation. And we would appear to be moved by their soul-stirring appeals, even to the shedding of realistic tears. Then when the ringing call would come for us to resolve to lead new lives, our hands would go up in eager unison, a gesture that was supposed to pledge our souls and minds to the straight and narrow path ever after.

They would leave the prison burning with the enthusiasm mighty things accomplished for the Cause. But if they could have heard our remarks following their departure I'm afraid they never again would have had the courage to face a prison audience.

These good but misinformed souls would spend much time and money in the prison crusades, and I suppose they still do so, but so far as my own experience can reach, I've never known a man who was reformed because of their well-intentioned efforts. *Personally I am convinced that a man changes his life pattern only when he himself is definitely ready for such a change. And that until he is ready, no pressure, reason or persuasion on earth can influence him one iota.* I am convinced, also, that reform is wholly a matter of transcending old desires and habits of life, and not the suppression of them through fears and other forces of the will. No man can claim to be reformed who is still in conflict with the old habits of his life. So long as such habits are not risen above, a relapse into them is constantly an imminent possibility.

But in spite of what I've found to be true in my own experience, I would not presume to set my findings up as a criterion. I have no desire to discredit or discourage the activities of prison social workers. Nor would I wish to discredit or discourage those engaged in the field of juvenile delinquency because of what I have experienced as a juvenile delinquent myself. It is important nevertheless, that I be honest in presenting my early attitude and conclusions as a youthful outlaw.

Naturally I came in contact with all the reform movements that were active at that time. If they taught me anything it was sharpness of wit. I soon learned that through these movements I could escape the consequences of much of my wrongdoing. I became an artful maker of promises and a skillful creator of lies. These I would trade for immunity whenever it could be done.

Quite often I was made the object for scientific study and treatment. These laboratory adventures, instead of helping me, served only to furnish another excuse for carrying on against whatever restrictive conscience I had left. They made me conscious of my difference from other kids. I was what I was because it had to be that way. I was born with a quirk in my brain. It wasn't my fault at all. Crime was just something that belonged to me; and any act I performed no matter how vicious was merely an expression of my natural self.

And later when the power of reason began to assert itself, I developed a cynical attitude toward all reform movements, I became skeptical of their motives, and even while I took every advantage of their influence, I resented their patronizing sentimentalism; their self righteousness; and particularly was I embittered by all psychiatrical attempts to dissect, analyze and label me in the manner of some queer zoological specimen.

Out of this resentment and bitterness grew the most deadly philosophy in the world. I call it convict philosophy. It contains the whitest logic ever conceived in the brains of men. It batters down every sham behind which people hide their weaknesses. It tears at all personal inconsistencies with tiger-like fangs. It makes all men, women and children criminals at heart; gives every one the impulse to kill, steal and ravage. To the criminal in prison it distinguishes but one difference between him and the person outside of prison, and that difference is enunciated with a sardonic sneer. The one is in, the other is out. That is all. A stone wall makes the only difference.

The danger of this philosophy lies in its very truth, for potentially and actually all men and women have come short of the law. The philosophy, also, has it self-condemnatory side. The criminal on the inside arraigns himself brutally for being fool enough to get caught in a trap others skillfully evade. After he is in for awhile he begins to see a hundred ways by which he might have escaped punishment. And he resolves thereupon never to make the same mistake again. And in this respect, at least, he leaves prison with good intentions, according to his own code.

All in all, the only positive thing that can be said about convict philosophy is that it is positively deadly to the man who entertains it. One who is inoculated with it is dogmatic to the point of fanaticism. He cannot be reached by either reason, punishment or persuasion, because his mind is set as hard as concrete against every attempt made to change him by those whose motives he questions. A prison sentence only adds fuel to the fires of his world-girdling disillusionment. He is a confirmed fault-finder, an absolute destructionist, and he seldom wakes up before it is too late to prevent his own physical, mental and moral decay.

*   *   *   *   *

During the time I was engaged in the following experiences—a period of three years, perhaps, in all—I made and preserved certain notes, a few of which I later published in a short series of brief articles. These together with the remainder lay fallow in my trunk for many months. Then they were shown to a friend, a man who had done something along the same line himself with, as he said, more or less nebulous results. He became quite interested and urged me to work my notes up in a book form. At the time I was unable to respond to his suggestions.

He thought that I was obligated to such a task; that I had no personal right to hide experiences of the kind. I, of course, was interested in his reasons.

"Why haven't I a right to keep them?" I prompted him.

He thought such a book might be helpful to others. Frankly my conceit was neither large enough nor my knowledge broad enough to include this reason. The knowledge I had gained, extremely meager though it was when compared to what I had failed to gain, had been sufficient to convince me that one man's experiences could do little more than stimulate interest in another; that they could not convince another of the efficacy in applying abstract principle to practical problems by merely reading about such experiences.

"That is a great service in itself," he said, "to stimulate, to encourage others to think for themselves and then apply their thinking to their own problems."

In his inimitably enthusiastic manner, he referred to me as one who had conquered an inferno. He said my methods had been practical and my accomplishments so obvious that merely to read of them would prove an inspiration to many with similarly difficult problems.

"In other words," I smiled at his fervour, "the world is in need of a brand new Messiah and you've picked on me for the job."

To my surprise and amazement he nodded his head. My smile became a hearty laugh. I the new Messiah! I whose numerous names adorned every police blotter in the country! I whose picture could be found in all the rogues' galleries, and whose measurements were tucked away in every bureau of criminal identification! I who had just recently emerged from a prison cell to point the way for honest folks to follow! I a burned-out burglar taking up the exemplary task of teaching ethics!

"It isn't so absurd," he said dryly. "There's been some pretty good men in prison cells, and there's been some pretty good things come out of prison. As I see it, it isn't that you were in prison that counts at all: it's what you did there that might be of help to some one else that really matters."

The upshot of it was that this friend convinced me finally that such a book might truly have some value as a contribution to human encouragement, if nothing else.

Certainly I approach the task humbly. My hope is that some of those in whose hands the book might fall will be moved to try the simple principles in their problems as I have been privileged to try them with highly beneficial results.

Throughout these pages I offer no false claims. There isn't a thing new or original between these book ends. In presenting what is as old as the universe itself, I haven't even the claim of an original literary style, whatever such a thing might be. I deal wholly in the obvious; but it is an obvious that for many years I refused to see, even to deny, and to continue to deny its presence until the scorching fires of prison hell had welded it into my soul.

I am not an author by any means. I am not even a very well educated person, having had practically no formal schooling. I am just a common ordinary human being who had to be taught horse-sense the hard way: by strong-arm methods.

The simple methods I have used were here with Adam. Many have used them before me. Many will use them after I've shuffled through the last dark door. All knowledge is a common property that may be appropriated, thank God, by those who need it and wish it. Knowledge is the one thing in existence selfish greed has failed to put a fence around and post with No Trespassing signs. Too, any intelligent person can do far more with a little knowledge than I have been able to do, for I am neither intelligent nor keenly receptive to the finer shades of wisdom and understanding.

As a plain matter of fact, I am handicapped with an overabundance of that sort of peace and contentment not attracted toward the ends of vigorous ambition. I am what some call a confirmed homebody. I'm satisfied with simple things: my books, my meditations, my thoroughly harmonious home, my club, my friends. I've entered the calm after the storm and I find it pleasant.

So far I've tried to use the creative principle with great determination only in the hard pinches; and if by recounting a few of these some of you are enabled to take another reef in your own flagging determinations, I'll consider my feeble effort repaid with multiple compound interest.

*   *   *   *   *

For about twenty years I used to engage in a most idiotic pastime. Like most criminals I had not yet discovered humour, so I took this pastime very seriously. I claimed as my pet aversion ignorance in everybody else, except of course, in myself. And since I had not discovered humour, my voice was raised in bellowing proportion against one particular form of ignorance. It goes without saying, I made a fool and a nuisance of myself. One of my most imposing defiance against this particular shade of ignorance, was a declaration of denial.

"If there's a God," I would roar heroically in the presence of some one whom I knew to entertain religious beliefs, "then let Him prove Himself by striking me dead."

Once I made the silly remark in the company of a

sardonic old safe-blower, who replied laconically: "God don't strike fools dead. He throws 'em a rope."

The droll remark came back to me when I had just about let out enough rope with which to hang myself.

I started out by hating God and wound up by hating everything, including my own infallible wisdom. I was a little too wise in those days to know anything about the psychology of hate and all other forms of negation. For example, I didn't know that hate could disturb the digestive and assimilative system to the extent of bringing on attacks of indigestion and constipation, sluggish blood circulation, and many other conditioning reflexes of the mind and body. I went right on suffering them all and hating. Besides it was popular in the circle in which I moved to evince the rebel spirit by hating all things sacred and decent.

I took great pride criticizing everything that did not conform to an attitude of destruction. As for human life, I held it in contempt. Nothing was cheaper, and nothing was so worthy to be preyed upon.

Consequently, being a criminal, and being so poor a criminal as to carry around with me a whole pack of defeatist's philosophy, I spent the greater portion of my time behind iron bars.

Now short terms in prison are not such terrifying experiences as most people imagine them to be. They terrify the beginner for awhile, but he soon becomes adjusted and settles down to make the best of things. It is the long prison terms that make of prisons a living death-house. When it's all said and done, there is just one punishment inflicted by prison incarceration, and that falls upon the long-termers. But this one punishment is sufficient to defeat any purpose the prison system might hold in the way of correcting criminal tendencies or eradicating criminal causes.

There is no normal outlet, physically, for the most purely animal dynamic force in existence; no normal way to gratify the most maddening hunger that ever gripped the human side of man; no way to turn the procreative impulse into normal human channels of expression. No way, that is, that prisoners have discovered, save a remarkably few. Only a very few have been able to sublimate this energy and turn it into useful purposes.

The usual attempted way, the vicarious way, and it represents all the ways possible to imagine, instead of gratifying the hunger only adds to it. Men and women in prison sacrifice themselves mentally, morally and physically to this relentless appetite without avail. Their sacrifices lead only to disgust with themselves; and occasionally it carries them on to a padded cell.

Otherwise, they are eventually released with the hope they are now purged of their pernicious tendencies. Such a hope is tragic in its pathetic disappointment. Wardens know it. All prison officials know it. But society doesn't know, because society would rather pay the bill, perhaps, than take an interest in such sordid facts. Such conditions do not and cannot prove beneficial to the social system. At any rate, such is my opinion. I'm willing to leave the matter in the hands of sociological students. So I'll go no farther into it here. I may even be wrong. It may be that these poor demoralized objects of an experimental penal age, are an asset to society. I prefer to think otherwise.

As I said before, the deputy warden came every morning to the door of my dungeon cell, tempting me to confess and go free. I held out doggedly for weeks. Emaciated and filthy, I was many times tempted to crawl to the door and accede to his wishes, but I always managed to steel my will against the course. As time went on the torture of starvation became less noticeable and less painful. Too, I felt myself gradually becoming inured to the cold. It seemed that my life was running out into a sort of dull, insensate chaos. Mine was a case of stubborn will versus the law of self preservation, with the former showing every indication of complete victory.

Why such a thought flashed across my mind I don't know—it had been years since I'd had a constructive thought—but there came to my soggy brain about this time a thought of wonderment. I wondered where such determination of will would end if it was directed differently, if it was turned toward a purpose of intelligent self interest.

There followed a period of mild, dreamy delirium in which I seemed to exist half awake and half asleep. For awhile the content of these dreams was like a confused and pointless riddle. They had no beginning and no end; but drifted and drifted and drifted through my head without continuity or consistency. As I grew weaker, however, they appeared to take on more definite outlines, to become more rational, more vivid and meaningful.

And then one day there occurred in my dream the man whom I'd been trying to hate for years, Jesus the Christ.

He appeared in a garden in every way similar to the one I had seen Him in as a child. His physical appearance was also similar. The whole picture had that quiet clarity about it that draws out thematic details of expression, of feeling, of thought, of purpose. He came towards me, His lips moving as though in prayer. He stopped near me eventually and stood looking down. I had never seen such love in human eye; I had never felt so utterly enveloped in love. I seemed to know consciously that I had seen and felt something that would influence my life throughout all eternity.

Presently, He began slowly to fade in the manner of some casual process of dematerialization. Out of what had been a vision of Him there emerged a vision of the word Love in large gossamer irregular letters, which remained a moment, and then as He had done, slowly vanished.

Following this particular dream I lay for a long time enveloped in a keen sense of awareness. Even though the visual aspects of the dream had disappeared, its quality lingered. It seemed to have become a part of me. Where I had been the recipient of the Master's love, I now felt myself exuding love. It seemed to pour from me in the form of some mighty sense of blissful gratitude, not for any one thing or things, but for all things, for life. I had no discernment or consciousness apart from this enchantment of universal love. I seemed to have escaped from all the personal bodily and environmental limitations that had hitherto tortured me. I was not aware of dungeon walls, but my thoughts seemed to roam afar both in space and time. In fact, neither time nor space appeared to have definition or the modification of boundary lines.

And later I became aware of still another sense of freedom. What I had always thought to be imagination, occurred to me as reality. While I visited places undoubtedly historical but ancient, I experienced no difficulty in adjusting myself to the modes and customs of these places. I seemed to possess infinite versatility, readily speaking the language or dialect of the various peoples of these places, and to be perfectly familiar with their laws, their religious beliefs, their government policies, their art and literature. In the reading of the latter, I seemed to possess an amazing proficiency. I read manuscripts and books by pages at a glance with an accuracy that was unerring.

By and by I became aware of my actual whereabouts, but not in the same sense I had been aware of it before. There was no sensibility of discomfort attached to the dungeon now, no feeling of bitterness or stubbornness. The place seemed to radiate with a wholly congenial and alluring atmosphere. My imagination appeared to function in an acute and consistently pleasurable manner.

I would experiment with the barren cell, reappointing it to fit the convenience of special guests, which I would later invite. Always these were men of wisdom, and always the dominating subjects discussed by them were subjects of life, and truth.

It was at these imaginary symposiums that I first heard of the creative principle, of the media of love, discussed in an analytical manner, which later, applied, not only opened my dungeon door without an overture on my part, but opened the front door of the prison for me long in advance of the time set by law for my release.

*   *   *   *   *

In trying to describe this state of temporary being, I'm not I desirous of being drawn into controversy about its causes or its scientific qualities or its lack of them. I am merely describing what occurred, its effect upon my future conduct and behavior, and what I was enabled to do with the knowledge I had gained in this manner. Nor do I wish to leave any egotistical impressions on the minds of my readers. I was lifted into this state through no conscious efforts of my own. It came to me unbidden, unsought. It was a gift to a man who, from the human standpoint, had rendered himself unworthy of human consideration. That it was an act of Providence I've never doubted. Why or for what purpose, I've been able only to guess. Left to my own devices my body soon would have been destroyed. I was doing all in my power to bring about that finale, and certainly the time for it was dangerously close at hand.

From the moment I was drawn into the state, unusual things began to happen. The prison doctor stopped at my door for the first time to inquire after my health, and to linger at my door and talk. He came three times in that one day, eager to do something for me in his professional capacity. Courteous and kind, he pressed me again and again for a different answer in regard to my health, and seemed bewildered when I reaffirmed the fact that I had never felt better than I did at the moment.

The keeper of the dungeon, a man who had taken a violent dislike for me from the start, came to my door with gracious words on his lips. I had hated him and now I loved him. He offered to disobey the rules and smuggle in a sandwich from the officers' dining-room if I'd only say the word. I thanked him, but explained that I was not in the least hungry. He went away shaking his head.

But during this period the deputy warden, who had been making regular daily visits to my door, suddenly stopped coming. Often I thought of him with an all-consuming compassion. I believe it was on the third day that he opened my door and said, "Well, buddy, I think you've had enough. You can go over to the hospital and clean up and rest for awhile."

A few days later I received a complete new outfit of clothing and was assigned a new and easier job in the prison shirt shop.

CHAPTER 3

Love Versus Prison Door of Self

Brave conquerors! For so you are
Who war against your own affections
And the huge army of the world's desires.
—Shakespeare.

We of today recognize the great English play-wright's genius, but what was taken for wisdom in his day we've found to be false in ours.

We know now that war in any form has never solved a human problem. We know that to declare a state of war between us and our desires does not eradicate those desires, but rather intensifies them in proportion as our war-like wills appear victorious and strong.

When I came out of the dungeon and had again resumed my routine duties, I was in possession of an idea that had worked a seeming miracle in my behalf. But while I had a recognition of this idea, I did not have the sense of illumination, the feeling of ecstasy that had been born to me as a result of it there. Too, although I realized the idea to be a medium through which I could contact creative power, I didn't know how to go about applying the medium to my problems now.

These problems were many and life-long duration. They began immediately to present themselves to me for consideration the same day I had my release from punishment; for that day there was established in me an intense desire for a new deal of livingness.

45

Therefore, I sat down one evening to list my mental, moral and physical assets and liabilities. I discovered that I had shelter, food and clothing, such as they were. I was able to read, write and cipher a little. Against these things the list of my liabilities ran into interminable lengths.

The problem appeared simple under such circumstances. I would simply start from scratch, and declare war on my physical ill health, replace my negative attitude with a positive attitude, substitute optimism for pessimism, and presto, all would be hunky-dory.

The thoughtful reader, however, will see that I had set a mighty big order for myself. In fact, what I desired to accomplish meant a complete right-about-face from all the destructive habits I had acquired and nurtured through the years. My intention was to go to war against them and slay them in one fell blow with the rapier of my will. My intentions were excellent; however, I hadn't reckoned on the strength of the enemy. My effort, though heroic, was short-lived and ended in dismal and mind-tormenting failure.

The more I tried to war against my habits, the more persistently they pressed their claims upon me. I grew melancholy under the strain. A sense of weakness and hopelessness took hold of me, which defied constructive thinking, which defied thinking of any kind, except thoughts of impotence and misery.

The desire for the things I had lived became more and more intense, until reason warned me that a compromise would have to be made, and compromise was the first step to failure. From it the plunge back down would be swift and certain.

But the worst of all, my health instead of improving under the ordeal, took an opposite turn. I soon learned that willpower was one thing, and that to use it constructively against life-long habits was another.

It seemed that all the legions of hell had turned out to concentrate their fire upon me alone. If I decided to miss a meal out of regard for my health, that particular meal would be certain to contain seldom-served items that I especially liked. Every time I picked up a magazine or newspaper, I would be sure to find some brilliant, logical attack up on the virtues I had set before me. Things occurred that I had never known to occur before to test my resolve. For instance, I had been an inveterate user of profanity. And being profane, I had not noticed it being used by others so much. But no sooner had I resolved to stop its use, I began to notice that every one seemed to use it. Books that contained it were thrust in my way. An essay by a popular author on the use of profanity was given to me. The author argued that those who did not curse had no strength of character. Men who couldn't say damn once in a while had lost all claim to masculinity. They were unpardonable sissies; and he clinched his argument with a long list of leaders in American history, including the father of his country, who had cursed their way to fame and victory over insurmountable odds. Profanity was a vigorous mode of expression that fitted perfectly into all occasions requiring force and vigour.

I had a habit of chewing tobacco, which, for me in prison, had been an expensive one to gratify. To obtain chewing tobacco had been a constant struggle. But now that I had resolved to give the habit up, the weed was forced upon me from all manner of sources without one single effort on my part to acquire it.

My strongest mental habit had been intolerance of other persons' opinions, which had, all my life, kept me in hot water, fights and squabbles. Of course, this habit headed my list. I determined I would look at the other fellow's viewpoint and respect it even if I couldn't agree with it. I would refuse to argue with anyone, taking the stand that fools argued and wise men discussed. But again this good intention was easier resolved than carried out. It seemed that those with whom I came in contact would be pacified with nothing short of hot words. And the more I tried to force my resolution by sheer will-power the more easily irritated I seemed to become.

I had always thought I possessed courage. I had no fear of physical pain. I had been clubbed by policemen into states of insensibility. I had faced death many times while pulling off burglaries; I would fight any man at the drop of a hat. Then one day, after I had made my resolution to be broad and tolerant, a fellow told me I was yellow; that I didn't know what courage was. I was on my feet in an instant. But I steeled myself, gulped down the old impulse to do battle, and listened while he brutally continued his accusation.

"I'll tell you what courage is," he said. "You've never known what the word meant. Everybody in this joint knows you've always been hard-boiled. You've preached tooth and fang sermons around here for years. Now you've decided you were all wet and wrong. You've gone wishy-washy. All right, if you've got courage you'll go up on the chapel platform the next day we have open forum and tell all your old friends all about it. Preach us a sermon about your grand and glorious reformation. That'll take the kind of courage you ain't got."

Strangely enough I hadn't thought of that particular kind of courage before. But now I realized that bullets and blackjacks were easier to face than the ridicule of one's cynical fellows *en masse*. As I pondered on such a predicament, I could visualize an audience of sneering faces; I could hear their cat-calls and boos; their hisses, and their innuendoes of turn-tail, yaller-cur, long-tailed rat, and a hundred other savage aspersions.

I didn't have the courage to face a thing of this kind, but I forced my will to accept the challenge. I made a prepared talk and committed it to memory. Then I sent my name and desire to the open forum director. I lived a million years of emotional agony between that day and the day I was billed to speak. When the day finally came I was almost a complete invalid. As I sat on the platform trying to pretend poise as the lines filed into the auditorium, the pit of my stomach was churning like a ball of red-hot vacuum without a mooring. As I was being introduced, a wave of nausea swept over me and I began to tremble from head to feet. As I rose, I was met with a roar of ridicule; tide after tide of it broke over me as I stood there waiting for it to subside. I felt as though I was losing consciousness. Then came a dead hush, in which I imagined one might hear a feather fall above the mad pumping of my heart. I started out to speak; my lips quivered open, but not a syllable issued forth. If ever self styled hero made an inglorious retreat that hero was me. I slunk from the auditorium amid the wildest surge of abuse I've ever heard before or since. Right there and then I decided to scuttle all my fine resolutions. But Providence once more came to my rescue, this time in a wholly different manner.

I was to occupy that same platform many times after this frightful fizzle. I was to debate my newfound philosophy of behavior with some of the most brilliant forum minds. *I was to hear cheers and applause, where I had once heard only sneers and guffaws. But I didn't achieve these things by the war process against my habits and weaknesses. I achieved then not by trying new habits that transcended the old.* To war against a thing is to hate that thing. To sublimate a condition is to employ the medium of love. The one compresses the condition into a more intensified circumference, the other expands it until it has no circumference left.

*   *   *   *   *

It so happened, and how fortunate it was for me, that just after I reached this crisis, I was transferred to a different cell! The man with whom I was to share this latter cell was a life-termer well along in years.

His name was Dad Trueblood, but he was often referred to as The Old Stir Bug. Ordinarily this name was applied in an uncharitable sense to those prisoners who had attracted it through odd or queer quirks in their mental characters. But in the case of Dad Trueblood it was untouched by the critical or opprobrious. For this old fellow was the most beloved man who had ever done time in this particular prison. He was loved by both prisoners and officials alike, a combination rarely found behind stone walls.

Dad was one of those exceptional persons the most chary could trust; one of those singular individuals who, without uttering a word, broke down the strongest restraint in others and set them to blabbing their troubles in his ear as naively as a child goes running with its troubles to its mother. He was one of those occasional men who could win another's confidence without effort, and with just as little effort keep that confidence strictly inviolable.

Had Dad wished to turn informer, he could have sent scores of his confidants to longer prison terms, and many to the electric chair. But Dad was not an informer, and although this prison, like all other prisons, was managed after the stool-pigeon system, no official ever thought of offending Dad's sensibilities by offering him special privileges in return for tainted favors.

The odd twist that gave Dad the name Stir Bug occurred because he had refused a pardon after having served twenty-seven years. His reason for such an unheard-of act was strange and yet wholly consistent with his character. When the warden asked him why he preferred to remain voluntarily in prison, he said that he was getting old; that he no longer had any friends or relatives on the outside; and that he thought he could be of more service in prison than out.

"But don't you want your freedom?" the warden had asked incredulously.

"I'm always free," the old lifer had replied. "It doesn't make any difference where you are on the face of the earth, warden. If your thoughts are free you're free. And there's no one can imprison your thoughts but yourself."

And so Dad Trueblood had been permitted the privilege of remaining a number instead of going out and once more becoming a name.

When I moved my belongings into his cell he was lying on his bunk. He welcomed me casually in a friendly manner. He knew, of course, of my reputation as a bad actor. There were few words passed between us until we had been locked in for the evening. Then I asked him if he had seen my fade-away in the chapel. Yes, he had been there that day. He thought most any one else would have done likewise under similar circumstances. But he asked no curious questions about it.

Finally, I related my experience in the dungeon; and of my desires after coming out; of terrific willpower battle to overcome my old habits; of my pitiful failure to do anything in that direction. "But after that chapel deal," I finished, "I got wise to myself in a jiffy."

"How do you mean?" he asked in an off-hand way.

"I mean this virtue stuff is all the bunk," I said.

"Then what does that make the other stuff? The stuff you've been living before?"

"There are some pretty wise men who have taken the gold out of the Golden Rule, and have made that rule look pretty small, at least on paper," I replied evasively.

"That doesn't seem important, son, in your case," Dad said. "You've been following another rule. The important thing is, what has it got you? Critics and logicians deal with the trees in a forest, without ever seeing the forest itself. That's what you should be looking at now—not the too logical details, not what the other fellow has done with your old philosophy, but what you have done with it. If you're satisfied with the results, then your rule has worked out, if not, then the sensible thing to do is to stick to your guns and try another way."

"But I've tried that and failed," I said hopelessly.

"No, you haven't," he said, "you've just gone at it wrong. For instance, if you wanted to become a cannibal right quick, where before you'd only been a moderate eater of meat, why just force yourself to break off with meat by using your will and nothing else. No, son, the easiest and safest way to rid yourself of many bad habits is to recondition yourself to one good habit. Once you have it established, the others will have disappeared without much strain."

What he did was to show me how to apply the idea I had discovered in solitary confinement, or rather the idea that had been discovered for me, and turned to my account in spite of me.

First I was to forget all about my notion of going to war with my habits. I was just to assume that nothing had happened to me; that my attitude was the same as it had always been; that I was not to make any attempt to force a change in my custom of living; but that whenever and wherever I could do it without strain or pressure, to do something constructively creative; a quiet thought, an encouraging word to some one at the right time, a stimulating hint to another, a constructive action, either selfish or unselfish.

I was to read, as I had always read, books that appealed to the negative side of my life. But as I read I was to try to build in something positive between the lines, whenever I could appear to do it without too much labor.

"Make it a game, son," he said, "and not a task. Let it be a challenge but not a command."

*   *   *   *   *

Guided safely by the unerring knowledge Dad had of sublimation, I entered into the spirit of the game and found it not only profitable but pleasurable. It was accepted as a novelty, a plaything, something, with which to while away the time; and the joy of which depended upon the game itself, and not upon the results to be accomplished.

During the day at my machine I made a game of sewing garments. Each one I finished had in it an effort to make it better than its predecessor. This part of the game alone relieved me entirely of the burden my labor had always had for me before. As I continued to play it, I soon found it becoming a fascinating habit. Time that had always dragged heavily with each begrudging stitch, now flew by on wings of tirelessness. I won privileges on my workmanship, and many compliments from the superintendent of the shop. But the surprising thing about it all was that I not only made better garments, but I was able to complete my task in much less time than when I had been fighting the sewing machine every minute and turning out slipshod material; where I had been constantly jerking at my cloth and breaking my thread, thus wasting time rethreading my needle, I now worked more smoothly and consequently with little lost motion. One of my best games was to see how many completed garments I could make without an accidental breaking of my thread. On several occasions I finished the whole task, twelve garments, without a mishap.

This game was taken up by those around me, and eventually spread over the entire shop. The superintendent was amazed at the results. He made it a competitive game and offered prizes for the winners. Not only were the garments made better; but there was a great saving accomplished by eliminating wastage, garments too hastily thrown together that later had to be discarded and new ones made to replace them.

And all the while I would be working away at my task, I also played a game with my thoughts. I would analyze them as they drifted through my mind. I would label each as it came along. If it was destructive, I would counter with a constructive one deliberately created for the purpose, and vice versa. As I continued to play, I soon became conscious of a subtle, but definite drawing away of the destructive thoughts. The constructive ones came more and more unbidden, until finally I was aware that whole sequences of them would pass through my mind without being broken by one negation. Too, I found it becoming increasingly repugnant to deliberately create a destructive thought to carry out my game of counteraction.

Then when my task had been completed, I hatched up another game. I called it the game of constructive deeds. Each day I tried to increase the number of little unobtrusive things I could do for my fellows. I would hold loving thoughts toward men who had always been my avowed enemies. Many of them I had bloody encounters with and hadn't spoken to since. Without fitting any other action to these thoughts, I watched and waited, and in every case was rewarded by seeing the iceberg melt that had stood between us, *and it wasn't long until I had no enemies left.*

This game by itself did something psychic to me. I didn't know what it was at the time. But it was an expanding something that drew men closer to me, even while I drew farther away from the life or the type of livingness they stood for. I didn't know why men distrusted the pious and self righteous sort of comradeship and fellowship; nor exactly what the difference was between that sort and the sort that I was expressing; but I knew there was a difference because the results were different. What that difference was didn't seem to matter. I was becoming more and more result-conscious, and this in itself was an excellent sign.

And then at night in my cell I would take up a book that I had always looked upon as my Bible. It was Schopenhauer's Studies In Pessimism. With this book I now made another fascinating game. I went through it thought for thought, translating it in long-hand on pieces of wrapping paper. My translation of the title was Studies In Positiveness. For each negative thought given by the author, I wrote down its best positive opposite.

Nor did one of the author's negations defy translation, indeed I invariably found many positive thoughts in one of his negative ones, from which I would choose the strongest. Sometimes it took me an entire evening to get over one page; other times I would do as many as five pages. Only once did I ask Dad to help me, and then he shook his wise old head.

"Solitaire is a one man game," he said, "and you're doing fine. Keep right after it 'til you win on your own efforts."

That enormous bundle of manuscript was destroyed. I've often wished I had preserved it. There was a certain sentiment attached to it, I suppose. It was something tangible that stood for something much greater, though intangible, the beginning of a slow but steady bulge upward. But after all, though the manuscript was destroyed, its effect on me is still alive and will remain so until the end of my days. The effects of constructive building are eternal: destructive building leads to limitation and death. But of all my early games with the implements of life, I believe this one, in its cumulative results, had the greatest influence for good.

*   *   *   *   *

The translating of this book gave me an intense interest in the positive side of life. It led me smoothly into an examination of the Old and New Scriptures, and of other literature that stressed the positive along with the negative in human behaviour.

However, in this prison at that time, true positive literature was a scarce article. One day I picked up a magazine of the kind that had been nearly worn out from much reading and had been discarded by its last reader. With great enthusiasm, I went through it from cover to cover. When I had finished I decided I would have a friend subscribe for it in my name and number.

The subscription was entered and I waited eagerly for my first copy. I waited several weeks. Then I had my friend write the publisher to find out about the delay. A reply informed me that the magazine, along with other printed matter from the same publisher, had been coming to me regularly. A little private investigation turned up the information that our chaplain, who was also our literary censor, had disapproved of the reading material presented through this publishing house.

My first impulse was to fly into a good old-fashioned fit of rebellion and write the chaplain a vituperative note of denunciation. In fact I did talk to Dad in no uncertain terms as to what I thought of a chaplain who would permit every deadening and salacious book and magazine printed to come in to us, and then set his objection on a magazine that didn't carry a single article or item not calculated to lift the consciousness of its readers.

The old man listened patiently until I had spent myself. Then he said: "All true, and heroically put, son. It's pleasing to unburden ourselves sometimes of what has all the earmarks of justifiable indignation. But the trouble with it in this case is that it only makes bad matters worse. Remember the little game you're playing? Well, it's a broad game. Any situation can be fitted into it. But not with hate and criticism; that is, if you expect to win."

"But how in this case?" I asked him.

"How did you break down enmity over in the shop?" He said no more. But his suggestion was enough.

I set about to formulate a new game around the chaplain. First I studied him and got to the bottom of his reasons for withholding my literature. I couldn't agree with those reasons. They seemed narrow and unreasonable to me. But I did grant him the right to entertain them, even though they had appearance of injury to me. I told myself that since the material printed in this magazine was in conflict with the religious creed held by the chaplain he was actuated by that consideration alone, and that he was honestly sincere in his belief that such reading matter would do harm to those who read it.

As I reasoned thus, I could not help but feel sorry for a man laboring under such rigid limitations. And this emotion, although it is not true love, is mighty close to compassion. At any rate, I soon found myself creating genuinely loving thoughts toward my censor. I began visualizing him as I thought the Master might visualize him. And the more I played at the game the more I thought of him as an expression of God and the less I thought of him as an expression of limitation.

Besides, I found a way of doing a few little services for him without his finding out who did them. For instance, I pointed out to my warder that three sun-shades would greatly improve the looks of the administration building. The warder agreed with me and said he would point the same thing out to the warden. As a result I was permitted to make the shades as well as the pattern. I made them as attractive as I possibly could; and they did improve the looks of that part of the building. But the one most pleased with the innovation was the chaplain, because it was the windows to his study they shaded against the afternoon sun.

On another occasion I was able to acquire a red-lettered student's Bible, a beautiful book, and have it placed on the chaplain's desk in his absence. On the first flyleaf I had written, "With the compliments of a friend."

In the meantime I spoke no word to him. I attended his services and found him saying things that were illuminating and admirable—things that I had formerly closed my mind against with a door of indifference and prejudice. With this door now opened the effect was exhilarating. I seemed to lose all interest in his human faults and shortcoming, particularly as they affected me. I began to think of him in terms of brotherly love and to feel what I thought intensely.

Then one noon day he came down the gallery and stopped in front of our cell. He carried under his arm several magazines and pamphlets that had been sent to me. He told me that he had seen fit to censor them because they dealt with pantheism, a dangerous doctrine. Recently, however, he had changed his mind and decided to allow me to have books, providing I would promise not to pass them on to others. I made no such promise; nor did he seem insistent on that point. I thanked him, and we talked for quite some time in a real get-acquainted fashion, and a friendship was there established between us that was active until the day I bade him good-bye.

This demonstration, and it was a demonstration, of the power of love to use creative principle effectively against adverse conditions, not only helped me in this particular, but it helped scores of my fellows, because shortly after it the chaplain lifted his ban on the literature of this publishing house and this prison became one among many into which this house sent free reading matter to the inmates.

*   *   *   *   *

Obviously, love can open prison doors—all manner of prison doors. But of all the doors most important to open, none is more important than the door of self. Self conquest through sublimation is the key to the fullest realm of livingness.

I do not presume to say that I had conquered myself. But I have traveled a piece of the way, and I am moving in the right direction. Looking down the list on the liability side of my ledger, I can see many items that have undergone a process of transformation and now adorn the side on which I've written down my assets. This side of my list is longer than the liability side, much longer. Many little victories have made it so, and each one of those small victories carried with it its own particular thrill. The game has been pleasurable and there is still much room for play. My asset list is only partially complete. I shall probably never complete it in my remaining lifetime, but I'll have a lot of fun playing the game to that end.

It will be recalled that at the time my list was made I suffered from many physical ills. These have all vanished without my being aware of the reconditioning process. Wholesome, constructive thinking did the trick, reflecting in my physical organism that which I held in my mind.

Since that time, and it has been several years, I've suffered very few physical indispositions. My body converts food into energy almost instantly now. I follow sane health rules, of course, for they are constructive and it pays to follow them. With excellent elimination and excellent assimilation, I am no longer a sufferer of that powerful physical enemy of man, inertia. I can work long hours without feeling fatigue. I can induce sleep within a moment and rest, perfectly relaxed for six hours, undisturbed by dreams or noise. All of which is something. Or at least to me it has been worth gaining, especially since the method used to gain it was a joy in itself. Cheerfulness to me now is a habit I seldom feel moved to break. Those long periods of hopelessness, indecision, worry, fear and lassitude are all over.

My greatest joy is obtained from playing my little game of deeds, of finding something I can do for others in a helpful constructive way. And although the joy is found in the doing, somehow these services have never failed to return good for good, in the same coin, only with multiplied interest, in the manner they were sent out.

As one of numerous instances of this kind, the case of Paul Harding comes easily to my mind. Paul was one of those many thoughtful, retiring boys who are frequently misunderstood, even by members of their own families, and who, as a consequence of this misunderstanding, often get off on the wrong foot for a start in life.

When I first knew Paul, I found him striving desperately to conceal his strong emotional life behind a front of callous pretense, sophistication, indifference, boredom. His efforts were pathetic. I saw behind these efforts the soul of a poet. And when I had broken away his false restraints, he admitted that as long as he could remember he had wanted to write verse. However, his early family life had not been conducive to or sympathetic with his ambition. Instead of constructive praise for his embryonic attempts, he had received ridicule, and this above all other forms of discouragement, is positively murder to a sensitive soul.

I promptly responded to his ambition and asked him to let me see some of his poems. He hadn't written any since he had been in prison, but with the interest I showed in his ability to do so, he produced a little poem in his cell that night, and strangely enough it displayed nothing of his pretense or the effects of his environment. It was a crude piece. Even I could see that. But the potential poet was there just the same. The theme of it was Pollyannaish. I advised him not to show it to any one else; for I well knew how it would be received and I also knew what such a reception would do for him. Instead, I encouraged him and set him to work writing more of them. And that was about the extent of my ability to help him. I knew nothing about the technique of verse-making.

When I told Dad about my predicament he laughed. "Well, you've got your foot in it," he said. "So you may just as well get a book on poetry and learn to write it yourself. That's the only way you can go any farther toward helping the boy."

And that is what I did. Paul and I studied verse-making together. And by and by we entered into a sort of competitive race. The idea was to see who would have his first poem published. Paul beat me with a fine little poem which was printed in his county newspaper. From then on he was a regular contributor to this paper, and later, before he left prison, a volume of his poems was brought out.

Now here is the way I profited through this bit of service. First, it was great fun. Second, I learned enough about it to be able to write topical verses and humorous verses, which I sold to magazines and newspapers under all kinds of names, and with the money acquired in this way, I was able to employ a lawyer for a friend who was innocent of the charge against him, a fact which was fully and completely established when his lawyer obtained a new trial for him.

This money was later returned by my friend with an additional sum and was promptly used over again towards the purchase of a community radio, the first one to be put into this prison for our sole benefit. And what a boon it was! Especially during the baseball season when we could get the returns of our favorite team play by play, instead of having to wait until the next day to read it all through stale news accounts.

I have said nothing about the real value of this poetry game as that value affected the life of Paul Harding. Need I say more than this: he gave up crime for poetry; he has prospered and so has society.

CHAPTER 4
Love Versus Prison Door of Ignorance

A boy is better unborn than untaught.
—Gascoigne.

There is one curse to which nearly all prisoners are subject, incomplete education or no education at all.

It seems almost inconceivable that only a few years ago a great institution such as the one in which I was incarcerated could have been without educational facilities for its wards. But such was the condition. Not only was it a condition, but it was a condition enforced by prison law. You were allowed to read such books as the library afforded; but to be discovered with a pencil or writing paper in your possession was equivalent to many days in solitary on bread and water.

One of the reasons institutional education was discouraged in this prison was because of an inferiority complex on the part of its officials. Under the prevailing wage scale for officials at that time, only a brutal and ignorant type of man could be induced to take these jobs; and these men found a mutual interest in ignorant prisoners; but in prisoners superior to them in education, they found a deep and abiding resentment. They were bitterly opposed to all forms of learning for prisoners that, by contrast, would tend to emphasize their own lack of learning. If a prisoner had been fortunate enough to have had the advantages of an

65

education, he soon discovered after entering the prison that he was in for hell, unless he was shrewd enough at the outset to conceal his educational assets by assuming a pose of ignorance. This was very often resorted to by educated prisoners.

Today this same prison has one of the finest educational systems in operation that has ever been established in any prison. (or it did have when I left there a few years ago). This school was functioning in conjunction with many big correspondence schools throughout the country. After the grades had been passed, the prison scholar could then avail himself of correspondence school training, which embraced everything in the way of vocation, and profession, from the arts and languages to business and the trades. Training was made compulsory up to the fourth grade; beyond that it was optional with the prisoner. It was a sight for earnest eyes to go into the big school room and see old men sitting side by side with youngsters mastering their A B Cs. And in another section of the room, to see eager hands trying to gain speed and efficiency on the typewriter; and in still other sections, to see competent inmate teachers patiently but effectively instructing their classes in all manner of specialties.

I do not say that this school is the finished result of any of my own efforts; but I can and do say proudly that because I had learned about the power of love to contact creative principle I was privileged to furnish the incentive or the nucleus around which the idea speedily grew.

Imagine if you can, an institution that for almost a hundred years had been managed on a system that exalted ignorance and low-rated knowledge. You would say that such a habit of management, ingrained by a century of unrelieved custom could hardly be uprooted in the course of a few months. That never-theless, is exactly what occurred.

Moreover, a college professor, a man of tremendous ability, was appointed to organize and superintend the difficult undertaking. He not only established the school, but he convinced those in power that a new school library was a necessary adjunct to a school of this kind, and thus for the first time in the prison's history the inmates could secure books of real educational value.

Of course, the idea first met with strong opposition both political and non-political. It required consider-able money to promote and realize an educational institution so broad in scope as this one. There were those who argued that education, instead of tending to correct criminals, would tend only to make of them a greater menace to society. A slow-witted criminal had little chance against the well organized forces of the law; but a criminal whose brain had been stimulated and developed through the process of education would be vastly more competent in the commission of crime. His imaginative faculties would become broader and more original; where he had once been dull, he would become clever; his ability to look ahead would be greatly enhanced, and thus he would be able to plan his crimes more efficaciously, eliminating the weak spots in his program of attack; where he had once blundered into his crimes blindly, without considering the most important feature in crime commission, the get-away, he would now be able to reason backward from a well-planned get-away to the crime's commission, a process of thought beyond the capacity of an ignorant criminal, but wholly within the powers of one whose mind had been trained in the difficult art of coherent, analytical thinking.

Students of penology watched the prison school system with much interest and speculation. Most of them were in accord with the movement. Most of them believed that the surest way to convince a man that crime was a losing game in the long run was to educate him to the point where he could see and understand this maxim for himself; and that the best way to create a potential good citizen out of a potential bad one, was first to arouse within him an intelligent self interest, and then place before him the means to cultivate that interest along constructive lines that entailed a knowledge of good citizenship and a desire to become a good citizen if for no other reason than the one based upon self preservation, that it paid to conform to existing social standards, even though to do so might often prove tedious and unprofitable.

Whether or not this controversy was ever settled I do not know. But this I do know, in my experience I observed more than a hundred confirmed criminals who, because of this prison educational system, left prison to fill honest occupations that had before been beyond their reach. Nor did I observe one among them who returned to prison for committing another crime.

*   *   *   *   *

It is my honest belief that if it is possible to reform a person of anti-social tendencies, there is no surer method to that end in existence than to turn constructively such a person, through education, away from the old tendencies by giving him new and more appealing ones to follow. There is a sense of *ought* in the most hardened criminal. Ought I to pull this job, or oughtn't I? These are the preliminary questions to every crime committed. And constructive education gives the constructive answer to them more influence over the individual by making that answer more reasonable and consequently more appealing. I believe penology's strongest weapon is education.

In this prison I was the first man ever to be permitted the unheard-of privilege of taking a correspondence course of study. At the time I had no idea how far-reaching the results of this privilege would be. And the warden, who granted me the privilege, of course established a precedent in doing so, and thus unwittingly let the bars down for an avalanche of similar requests, which he could not refuse, and which absolutely snowed him under.

He was bewildered when he called me into his office. "I've made a mistake in letting you have that course," he said. And then he pointed to a ten-inch stack of requests. "They're all the same. Fellows wanting to order courses. We have no mailing facilities here for handling so much of this type of stuff. I'm afraid I've got my foot in it. I didn't know there was such a craze in the world for education. God only knows how I'll ever get out of it."

I knew, of course, that one of his ideas for *getting out* was to backtrack on the original privilege granted me. I had to think fast in order to forestall this action. So I said:

"Warden, here's your chance to contribute a real service to society. It'll never pass your way again. If you seize the opportunity now, your name will go down as one of the outstanding prison executives of the world; but if you let the opportunity slip you'll pass out with the next change of administration, just another prison warden who served his time and drew his pay as wardens have done before him. Why don't you put in a school? Get a good man in charge of it and let him handle it in his own way. In that manner the problem will solve itself so far as you're concerned."

"By Jove!" he exclaimed. "That's an idea. I anticipate a fight. But I'm ready to go to the bat."

And with that vigorous statement a hastily formulated dream of mine had its first push forward toward fruition.

When I first thought of asking the warden for the privilege of taking a course of study, I was fully aware that such a request, under ordinary circumstances, would he briefly received and flatly rejected. Dad Trueblood and I talked the matter over, and as always, Dad had only one method for attacking all problems— the method of contacting creative principle through the intermediary of love.

"But how am I going to reach the warden? How am I going to make my love known to him?"

"Love," he said, "needs no advance agent. When it's purely conceived and powerfully felt, it will find its objective. It does not follow you: you follow it. First you love, and then you act."

"You mean I can prepare the warden in advance so that he will receive my request with favor?"

"Not you. But love expressing through you will prepare him."

"Without any effort on my part?"

"None but love. In fact, you need not go about him at all. Say, that's an inspiration. Instead of you making the request of the warden, let your friend on the outside do it, by mail."

Contrary to general opinion, it isn't so difficult to evoke a feeling of love even for one's jailer. You can reason yourself into this emotion. That is what I did in this case. And it worked out perfectly.

After all, I said to myself, prisons were a necessary evil in a civilization that harbored the type of preying animal I had been. And if prisons were necessary, so were wardens to manage them. This warden was merely filling an inevitable duty, and if it wasn't him then it would be someone else. Despite the disagreeable position he held, he was a man for all that, with the same God-given spark that I possessed, the same potentialities for good and evil. We were brothers under the skin. We were both headed in the same direction, although our paths had not always run parallel. He had his troubles the same as I. His faults were no worse than mine. In a word, he, as every mortal born to struggle up through trial and error, was more entitled to love and understanding than to censure. Who was I to sit in judgment? Had not the Master of men said, "Woman where are thine accusers?" And refused to judge her Himself when He noted all had slunk away.

In this manner of reasoning one unavoidably comes to the place where censorship ends, and where censorship ends true love begins.

It took me only a very short while to arouse within me a deep responsive feeling of love for the warden, and it grew and grew as I continued to search his inner being for the Christ-like traits that were the heritage of every human being.

Finally I began to visualize him in all manner of constructive, humanitarian activities. I saw him courageously doing the right thing, although he well knew that the right thing was not the popular thing for him to do. I saw him with my request in his hand; I sympathized with him when he passed through a wavering period of indecision; I bowed in inward gratitude when his eyes took on the light of victory over self and indecision fell away from him as he determined to do the constructive thing and allow me to have my course of study.

In the meantime I had written to my friend explaining my desire and asking her to inform me of the exact hour and date her letter to the warden was to go forward. In this manner I was able to arrive at the date and hour the letter would reach the warden's desk. Through another source I found out the exact time the warden sat down to examine his mail. And thus at this time I visualized him with my friend's letter in his hand. As I watched him reading it, I let my love close in around him until he seemed to be completely enveloped in it to the exclusion of every other vibratory influence.

I would not say this was scientific procedure. Some of you may even laugh it off as being the antics of a simpleton. I wouldn't presume to state that such an effort on my part had anything to do with the warden's decision. But I do say that his decision was made precisely as I wanted him to make it.

*   *   *   *   *

Through this course of study I was able to prepare myself for an honest, constructive future. I left prison at a time when the depression had just reached its peak, when competition in the labor market was as great as it ever has become. It might be that without this preparatory work I could have gone out in the world and competed successfully with skilled and unskilled millions. It might be that my prison and criminal record, all that I possessed in the way of reference, would have offered no handicap to me in my effort to secure a place in the world of honest endeavor.

But in the event the situation had not panned out in

this manner, which would have been at least quite possible—what then?

Maud Ballington Booth once wrote a book under the title *After Prison, What?* A man may go out of prison with the very best of intentions, but if he is unprepared, if he is worse off than when he entered prison, his intentions are likely to meet with opposition too strong to be endured. Nothing will so take the starch from an ex-prisoner's stiff resolutions like rebuff and indifference. As soon as he becomes thoroughly convinced that he is not wanted, the step between that point and his old life becomes a mighty easy one to take.

I remember a resolution I once made of the kind as I was leaving prison after serving my first term. I had been given a parole. The town I went to on parole had a shoe factory in it, and by telling a few skillful lies I managed to get a job in this factory. It was a good job, too. It paid excellent wages on a piece work basis. And the novelty of earning an honest living had a certain appeal about it, which I responded to with considerable satisfaction.

In the evening after a good bath and hearty supper I would stretch out on my bed and declare to myself, "By golly, this is not so bad." There was a definite lift to this business of achieving a laudable day's work; a decided sense of security about it that was wholly new and tremendously gratifying. If the thing hadn't happened that did happen shortly afterwards, I might have, then and there, reconditioned myself to honest habits of a lasting nature.

But one noon-day, as I hurried up the street from the factory on my way to a restaurant, someone hailed me from across the street, using a name of mine that sent a tremor of fear through me. No one in this town knew me by that name, or so I thought. Turning I saw a detective coming across the street to greet me. It had been he who had arrested me for the crime I had just finished a prison term to expiate. His face was aglow with a broad smile. His hand was extended in friendship.

"Glad to see you out," he exclaimed. "When did it happen? What are you doing?"

I explained I had been out several weeks; that I was on probation, that I was working down at the shoe factory.

"Fine," he said. "I for one am with you one hundred percent. I want to see you make good. Listen, just lay off the pool halls and other joints around here, and you'll pull the grade. I'm here now. I'm with the railroad. Dammit, if the sledding gets tough, come out to my house. We'll make you acquainted with the right sort of people. There's no need for you to get lonesome."

I was amazed at the man's attitude. I wondered if I had previously misjudged him. I returned to the factory feeling a little relieved but shaky in the region of my solar plexus. I had been at work about an hour when I was notified the superintendent wished to see me in his office. I felt the old sardonic sneer welling up in me. I remember saying to the floor boss who conveyed the message to me, "Well, I guess this is the end of a perfect day. A minute later, I was asked if I had ever served time in prison. Of course, I well knew who had informed on me. The detective had gone straight from his Judas kiss to the superintendent and advised him that an ex-convict was in his employ.

I admitted the fact with a sarcastic barb at the

whole world. The superintendent was sorry that the rules of the company forbade, and so forth.

"You needn't be," I told him. "I'm out of place here anyway. I'm glad I got by long enough to buy a good gun. That's my racket. It's all I know. Give me my check and I'll be out on my way in a jiffy."

I walked away from that job with a poisoned heart and a bitter resolution eating into my brain like a cancer. It took some time to dull the edge of that mood. In the meantime I did some reckless things against the social order before I finally stopped with another prison sentence.

$$* \quad * \quad * \quad * \quad *$$

I have said elsewhere that reformation to be effective and permanent must be accomplished by transcending old habits; by reconditioning one's self to new habits of thought and behavior.

To this end the average prisoner will neither respond to reason nor persuasion, harsh treatment nor kind. But, quite to the contrary, he will readily respond to an educational program with an inspirational tone to it, the quality that arouses self interest, and offers a positive means to a broader mode of living for him. When such a program fails, the man is hopeless so far as human influence is concerned. Nothing save an act of Providence can swerve him from his downward path.

As an illustration of what education can accomplish where all other methods have failed, I wish to recount, briefly, the cases of two men, not because I was privileged to play a minor part in their salvation, but more to show that even the worst of human timber can be salvaged from the gulf of destruction and rendered useful to society when the educational method has been made available to them.

Spider Ross was young in years, but old in experience. He was one of those borderline cases the criminologists like to study. That he was criminally insane the doctors had no doubt. But always convictions for crime and sentences in Spider's many mishaps sent him to prison instead of the criminal insane asylum.

Spider was one of those shifty-eyed, loose-lipped, pasty-faced crooks of the petty variety. A kleptomaniac, I believe they call them in professional terminology. He could neither read nor write his own name. He walked with the swaggering defiance of ignorance, and so far as any one could judge from mere observation, he possessed nothing but a surface, and a shallow surface at that. Apparently his only ambition was to live his own life and be allowed to brag about it as he liked.

When the prison school was established, Spider of course became what they called a "list man," that is, his name was on the list of those to whom training was made compulsory. I worked beside Spider, and when he heard they were going to force him to attend school, he promptly revolted. "I'll go," he told me, "but they can't make me learn anything."

It didn't take me long to realize that the school could be of little service to Spider so long as he held this attitude. I took his problem to the school superintendent and asked him to allow me to handle Spider's case. He agreed to my request, and I thereupon removed Spider's name from the list. When the list-bearers made the round to notify the others the day school was to start, Spider was passed up. Though he said nothing, it was plain he had taken the event as a slight and was very much disappointed. He wanted to tell the list-bearer a mouthful, as he put it.

The school was a roaring success from the start. In the shop there was no other topic of conversation. Enthusiasm ran riot. Spelling matches were begun; arithmetic problems were pondered over and solved. Every one had a stack of school-books he carried back and forth. The more literate prisoners turned from topics of crime to topics of history, government, economics, and so on. World's Almanacs were borrowed from the new library with which to settle disputes. Spider found himself completely disassociated from his fellows. Everywhere he went the conversation had to do with school subjects. After the tasks were all in, the prisoners would form groups, each on its own intellectual level, and get off in a private place to discuss their next day's assignments. If Spider approached one of these groups he would remain only a moment, because he had no mutual interest there. It was practically a case of unintentional ostracism.

Spider was in the position where "a feller needs a friend." And his extremity proved my opportunity. When he could talk to no one else, I talked to him as we worked. I talked to him about the thrill one got from trying to learn things. Slowly but surely, his interest rose. Then one day he asked me why they had left his name off the school list. I replied by suggesting that he must have requested it. He was vigorous in his denial of this.

"Well, I guess they figured you weren't interested in school," I countered.

"I don't see why," he said, "I didn't say so."

"But maybe they figured you thought so. Actions speak louder than words sometimes, you know."

He wondered if it was too late to get in. I thought I

could arrange it for him. But he would have to study hard in order to catch up with the rest.

And so Spider Ross the next day found himself for the first time in his life on the inside of a class room. No doubt he was an exception, but once he was started and had mastered the first difficult steps, after he had learned to read a little, his thirst for more knowledge became an exaggerated mania, the talk of the prison. In two school terms he absorbed what was equivalent to an eighth grade education. Every one was amazed at his capacity to assimilate complicated subjects. He was never without a book within his reach. As he operated his machine the book stood propped open before him.

At the beginning of this third school term, he took up business, shorthand and typing in conjunction with a correspondence course in salesmanship. At the close of the term he was placed in one of the most difficult stenographical positions in the prison where question and answer dictation had to be taken with the speed of a court reporter. While holding down this job, he found time to continue his studies, to invent a dozen or so different kinds of gadgets, which he planned to copyright later, and to write two excellent books on salesmanship, one under the title *The Psychology of Depression* and the other, *Depression Salesmanship.*

Spider left prison in the midst of the depression. His methods for making personal capital out of national hard times were all set forth practicality and convincingly in his books. That he demonstrated his theories, I haven't the slightest doubt in the world, although I heard nothing more of him after he had taken his departure.

I reiterate, his was doubtless an exceptional case. When a man can start from the lowest level of ignorance and criminal insanity, and in three years' time win a place of position of trust within his prison, and prepare himself as he did for a position of trust outside his prison, such an achievement is not only exceptional, it is phenomenal.

The important thing is, however, that he did it. The important thing to society. Institutional education had taken an obvious social menace in Spider Ross and transformed him into a social servant. Thus I have found it: education lifts the consciousness of the prisoner it touches, instead of contributing to the furtherance of his criminal tendencies.

And again we see in Spider's case, how first there was developed an intense thirst or love for knowledge, which set the creative principle to building in an opposite direction. Before his love medium had been for destructive things and such things had been created through him. With the love medium reversed, the creative principle could do nothing else but create in the new direction. As the love medium tends the creative law inclines.

*   *   *   *   *

The case of Harry Simmons was quite different from that of Spider Ross in one way, but the result was similar in that through the prison school both had been able to find themselves and their particular niches in life.

Harry had attended college, was an excellent scholar and possessed a high standard of taste toward the cultural things. He could discuss academics with a glib and perfect accent. He was typically a young intellectual, a trifle egotistical, somewhat snobbish, and vastly intolerant toward those whose frontal bones failed to measure up to the lofty dimensions of his own.

At some point in his educational career he had come under the influence of a certain German philosopher. This philosopher propounded a super-man doctrine which, in the hands of a person more impressionable than stable, held a dangerous interpretation, an interpretation altogether ruthless and inhuman. Indeed, it was Harry Simmons' misinterpretation of a brainy man's philosophical doctrines that paved the way for his pride to prison.

"Live hard and dangerously," was the credo this philosopher laid down for the guidance of the super-man. Meaning, of course, that it was the duty of the super-man to dare the faggots of ignorance by living and teaching in advance of his time. Poor Harry thought the philosopher meant that the super-man, being so brilliant as to appreciate the shortness of mortal life, should crowd into it as much vice and merry-making as he possibly could.

So he became a hard and dangerous liver. He naturally found such living expensive. At first he gambled for the wherewithal; and later he tried forgery. After his parents had bankrupted themselves trying to keep him out of prison over a period of several years, they were finally obliged to stand aside and see their prodigal take it on the chin for a five years' stretch.

Harry had what they called a political job in our shop. He wore a white shirt instead of the regulation hickory. He was a garment checker and shipping clerk. He was not liked because of his highbrow attitude and he was difficult to reach because of the thick veneer of know-it-all-ness he had drawn about him.

At any rate, I decided that Harry had too good a start in life to let himself drift down the purple tide and wind up in his old age a doddering prison lag, sitting around in the idle house of his final prison home spinning yarns about his many exploits, and comparing the conditions in this prison to the conditions in that one. But while I made up my mind to attack him with the weapon of love, I decided at the same time to use argument, since he loved to argue above any other pastime.

I crossed verbal swords with him one day with an introductory remark that set his blood boiling.

"Say," I said, most unexpectedly to him, "what do they teach guys like you in college?"

"To mind their own business for one thing," he shot back.

"Oh, I thought they taught them to write checks on the old folks' bank account."

"Is that so! Well, get an earful of this. They also teach them how to use their fists, if you happen to think you're lucky."

"I don't resort to violence," I said with a broad grin on my face. He promptly thawed out, and we were soon talking about his favorite topic, the philosophy of the super-man. We argued off and on for several days before he was willing to accede to my constantly reiterated point that any philosophy was a failure, unless the person embracing it could show that it had done him good instead of harm.

After drawing this admission from him, I pointed out that the same thing could be said of a college education; that although college men had a great advantage over non-college men, the latter by making opportunity out of the little they had, often succeeded in life, while the college man who refused to see the opportunity in the much possessed, failed in the practical business of life, that of growing and getting ahead.

These discussions, carried on at odd times daily, created a mutual bond between us, a thing that I had been working for, because I wanted to touch upon a most delicate subject later on, one that only friendship could take without resentment. I wanted to show him and make him realize what he had done to his parents, especially his mother, by dragging down the many excellent opportunities they had made possible for him.

He told me later that I was the only person on earth who could have brought these things home to him without giving offence. He was glad I had done it. Also, for the first time, our discussions made him conscious of the fact that, instead of copying his favorite philosopher's virtues, he had been twisting those virtues into vices and copying them.

As you probably have already divined, Harry Simmons had scoffed at the idea of a prison school for convicts. He had said that ninety per cent of the guys in this prison were too dumb to learn anything if they were kept in school a million years. He had evinced a great pity for the poor boobs who would have to act as teachers. He had also said that was one job he would not do under any inducement or pressure. He preferred the dungeon to such a job.

But Harry Simmons did become a teacher in the prison school. He sought the job, and he filled it in an exemplary manner. He had a Spanish and English class that positively worshiped him. He became the professor's most valuable assistant and he, more than any one else, was responsible for some of the finest features that the school possessed. In a word, he became a prison school enthusiast, and served the cause early and late to make it an outstanding success, and in this way squelch the criticism that still rumbled ominously here and there.

On commencement days, held in the big auditorium, with many noted educators from various places present to study the effects of the system, it was Harry's privilege to make the address which outlined the accomplishments of that semester and voiced the hopes of the one immediately to follow, for this school had only a very short holiday period.

How different was the philosophy this boy propounded in these addresses to that which he had brought with him to prison! He was like a new creature. As he would warm with enthusiasm, he was like a man who had caught a powerful vision, and was eager to convey the inspiration of it to those who were still floundering about in search of themselves, as he had been.

Harry was not a pupil in this prison school seeking an education, but he got about as much out of it as any pupil there. It was not education he obtained, but re-education.

Harry was still there when I pulled out. But he's gone by this time, and I would be willing to wager a goodly fortune that he'll never go back to that prison or any other.

One of the best debates the forum ever promoted was between Harry and an equally brilliant fellow on the philosopher Nietzsche. As I sat and listened I glowed inwardly with gratitude when the youngster revealed to me he had at last gotten close to the real Nietzsche and had reasoned away the shadow he had been following of that greatest of all original thinkers.

CHAPTER 5
Love Versus Prison Door of Violence

Whoever lives true life, will love true love.
—Browning.

According to the law, to have guilty knowledge of a crime, before or after, makes you equally guilty, providing you fail to divulge that knowledge to the proper authorities. On the other hand, according to the unwritten law of the underworld, to divulge knowledge of a crime makes you guilty of informing, and the penalty for this is death.

I believe there is such a thing in the universe as the law of Personal Position; that there is a right and wrong place to be at any given time; that if you are in your right place you will have nothing to fear in the way of attracting adverse compensation; but that every time you put yourself in a place where you have no business to be, a penalty of some kind will be exacted.

It was through no intention to be nosey or curious that I found myself in the following predicament; but since law is no respecter of good or bad intentions, ignorance, or any other excusing circumstances, I was faced with a situation that looked anything but pleasing.

There was a stock room in the shop where I worked in which all the supplies were kept. If a machine operator happened to ruin one of his pieces, it was his business to call the supply man, apprise him of his need, and wait at his machine until he brought an extra piece to replace the ruined one.

On this occasion I had attempted to re-notch one of my collar bands and had cut too deeply into the cloth. I looked around and not seeing the supply man about the floor, I thought I might save time by going in search of him. I got up and strolled back to the stock room. Noticing the door partly ajar I went in with the intention of serving myself. While I was carrying out this notion, from the other side of the supply bins the subdued sound of three voices reached me. They were plotting an escape. I knew the owner of each voice. And before I could make a quiet departure, I learned that the plot involved the lives of two men, one a guard, the other a prisoner.

I got out of the room and back to my machine. But I had been seen by one of the plotters who had not been present at the session just described, but who was aware that such a session was in progress at the time I entered. This man's suspicions were immediately aroused and he promptly labeled me a spy, hoping to gain information whereby I might feather my own nest, possibly gain my own freedom at their expense.

It was one of those situations in which many a prisoner has found himself and from which many a prisoner has died mysteriously without the prison authorities ever learning who did it or why it was done.

As soon as possible this fellow conveyed his knowledge and suspicions to the leader of the plot, a man with a tough reputation and a desperate desire for freedom. For obvious reasons, I cannot use the leader's name here, but for convenience I shall refer to him vaguely as Muggs.

For some reason, a very fortunate reason, by the way, for me, Muggs decided upon a course of action different from that usually pursued in such cases. Instead of remaining silent and keeping me in ignorance of the fact that they were aware I had knowledge of their plans, Muggs called me to one side and said:

"I ain't never knowed you to snitch; but I do know you've gone hay-wire since you done that last jolt in the hole (dungeon). We're goin' on through with this, an' you're goin' with us—or else! You've declared yourself in, an' now you're gonna stay in."

Without hesitation he informed me of the part I was to play. Also, if there occurred any hitch in their plans, he made it unmistakably clear that I would be held responsible.

During the noon hour one prisoner, a trusty, was allowed the privilege of remaining in the shop instead of having to return to his cell after lunch. Now that I was one of the plotters, there were five of us in all, one of them being the fellow in charge of supply room. Just before time to line up for the noon march to the mess hall, this man was to pass us into the stock room unobserved, where we would hide until the rest of the prisoners had filed out, and the guard had gone to the officers' dining room for his lunch. Then when the trusty had returned from the mess hall and entered the shop, we were to capture him, perhaps kill him if it was later thought advisable. Likewise we were to follow the same procedure when the guard again put in his appearance.

The captured or killed guard was to be disarmed and stripped of his uniform, which I was to don. Then Muggs, with the guard's gun on my back, followed by the other three plotters, was to march me in front of them to the back wall gate, where I would order the wall guard to throw down his gun and the gate key, it being presumed, of course, that he would mistake me for one of his fellow officers. In case the wall guard became stubborn he was to be shot from his perch with promptness and dispatch.

Had there been within me a desire for freedom in the same degree as this desire actuated the plotters, I should have still deplored their methods in attempting to obtain it. Every item of their plot was based upon violence and the crudest sort of violence in the bargain.

While I could plainly see a dozen different weaknesses in their scheme, any one of which, after murder had been committed, would have made their capture inevitable and their ultimate death in the electric chair an absolute certainty, they could not see these flaws, because they had permitted their objective to blind them to everything but the objective itself.

I was soon made to understand by Muggs that my advice was unsought and unwelcome. My position in the plot was not to reason why, but to do or die. Certainly I was on the spot, to use the vernacular. At this moment only one course was open to me, and that I promptly rejected, not because of fear but because of principle. Of this principle there are grounds for a wide divergence of opinion. Some may think it lacked what a moral principle should have, the sense of duty toward others, and that it was my duty to inform the authorities that such a plot was being hatched and the lives of two men and possibly three were being threatened.

I wish to make plain my attitude, therefore, and to make clear the objection I previously mentioned regarding the use of violence.

Had I turned informer against my fellow prisoners, that act in itself would not have embraced violence, but it would have resulted in violence. Those against whom I informed would have been subjected to third degree methods in an effort to make them admit the plot, or to confirm any information. But this would not have been the end of violence. By and by I would have had to reckon with the men I had betrayed; either I would have to kill one or more of them in self defense, or be killed by them. In the meantime my act of treachery would have brought down upon me the frightful curse of ostracism, and would have thus destroyed the influence I had begun to exercise for good among my fellows.

Luckily there was one man I could trust to share my secret in return for his advice, my old reliable cell-buddy, Dad Trueblood.

The old man admitted that I was in a ticklish place between two fires. "But," he added, "there never was a problem that could not be solved by love, and this one is no exception."

To this I agreed. But I could see no way to induce more love than I already felt for these men. Because I was able to see clearly what they could not see, my sympathy for them was vast. Yet they had not and apparently would not respond to it to the extent of allowing me an equal voice in the plot.

"You'll have to get their confidence through the voice of action," Dad said. "You'll see, you're no longer in their class. They look at you as one who has gone the reform route. You've got to make a sacrifice and make it appear that you've gone hard-boiled again. You've got to get yourself in trouble and go to the hole. I'll fix it up with the warden."

"But I don't want the warden to know of it," I broke in quickly.

"Of course you don't. Do you think I'd be that big a fool. I'll tell him you have a different reason. He knows you're using all kinds of schemes to help guys in here. I doubt if he'll even want to know a reason."

Thus one day a short while later, I surprised the entire shop by refusing to work. The guard's duty, of course, was clear. He told me three times to return to my machine. I argued with him in a loud angry voice that every one could hear. I thought for a minute I was in for a hard blow on the head, as the guard became angry himself at my display of insolence. He told me a fourth time to go to my place or he would send for the man (deputy warden), and I told him to go ahead.

While I waited for the deputy to show up, I strolled down the floor past Muggs' machine. Out of the corner of his mouth he said:

"Don't weaken. They can't do any more than give you the works, an' they ain't gonna do that."

"Don't worry," I replied, "their hole don't bluff me any. I've been in it plenty of times."

"What's the matter?" Muggs asked.

"I just ain't feeling good today is all. And they want me to work any way. They can lead a horse to water but they can't make him drink."

I put in fifteen days on bread and water and was then sent back to work. The price I paid to gain a point was pretty stiff. But when you consider the fact that my gesture doubtlessly saved the lives of several men, the cost will appear small indeed. The point I gained was, of course, the mutual respect and confidence of Muggs and his fellow plotters. With this confidence and respect I was given a voice in their plot councils, and in this manner I had no difficulty in pointing out the weak spots in the whole scheme, the hazards involved, and the inevitable consequences incumbent upon failure. In other words, I was able to reduce the plot to glamourless realism, and after I had accomplished that the desire for freedom had lost about ninety per cent of its erstwhile appeal.

All of these men served out their terms in the slow but safe way. I had convinced them that, while freedom was a wonderful prize to win, violence was a dangerous method through which to gamble for it.

One of the strong arguments for institutional education is that it tends to eliminate prison plots of violence. Any plot entering the mind of an ignorant person fails to bring with it the fine points in execution that the same plot brings when it enters the mind of a person trained to reason and analyze. Most of the prison uprisings are conceived in the childish brain of one man whose original motive is an abnormal desire to gain notoriety and thus bask for awhile in the limelight and adulation of his equally ignorant and subnormal fellows. Occasionally an educated prisoner or criminal is forced, through the intervention of unexpected circumstances, to resort to violent methods; but such methods are seldom a part of his original plans.

When an educated prisoner plans an escape, he goes about it in a scientific manner. He works through a process of elimination, and the things he eliminates are all the possible features that might compel him into an act of violence. He plans intelligently for success; but in case of failure he doesn't wish to be faced with the grim prospect of having to pay for a string of violent actions.

Prison officials fear the shrewdness of their educated charges; but they never fear for their lives in dealing with them.

*   *   *   *   *

By employing the love medium, I was able to save several men from such consequences as would have befallen Muggs and the rest of us had their ill-planned plot gone through. The following case will show how much easier it is to reach an educated person under similar circumstances. But again I must refrain from using the man's name. Therefore we shall merely call him Frank.

In this case I was taken into Frank's confidence without having to inveigle my way in through trickery or persuasion. Frank had been plotting his escape for several months. Finally he arrived at the place where he thought he had reduced the plot to its ultimate perfection. He could search through it from beginning to end and no flaw would appear.

And still—and here is the difference between an educated man's plotting and the plotting of an ignorant or partly educated man—although Frank could pick out no flaw in his plot, the intuition that goes with intelligence, warned him against becoming too cocksure. He had been close to his plot for a long time. Perhaps he had been too close; so close that some apparently trifling detail had escaped his notice; and this very detail might be the one glaring flaw, if he could only get far enough away from his plot to see it.

So far Frank had planned alone, another characteristic of the educated prison plotter. Frank and I were the very best of friends. The reason he had failed to confide in me before was not because he feared to trust me, but because he feared I would attempt to dissuade him from carrying out his intention. He came to me now and laid his plans out, knowing full well that I would scrutinize them with a fresh mind and expose any weaknesses that he himself had been unable to find.

He had obtained a small piece of an old file. With this and a knitting needle he had made a pick with which he could unlock the window to the shop machinist's cage and thus reach through to a tray of hacksaws entrusted to the machinist's care. His idea was to watch the machinist in the evening when he checked his tools in the presence of the warder; after which he would wait for an opportunity to act unobserved, unlock the window and possess himself of one of the saws, and then relock the window. With the saw and a bolt of shirt cloth, which he intended to smuggle from the shop, his plan was to cut the bars on his cell, climb to the top of the cell block, cut a padlock on one of the big ventilating cupolas, and through this make his way to the roof, where he would make fast one end of his cloth rope and slide to the ground.

"Your plan is all right, Frank," I told him. "But suppose it doesn't work. There's always an element of chance in the most perfectly planned getaway, you know. What if you fail?"

"Well," he said, "I'll just go to the hole for a few days. I don't expect to injure anybody; so if I do get caught it won't amount to much."

"You haven't considered the machinist," I replied. "He's in here for murder, and if I were you I wouldn't want to take much of a chance on his temper."

"Why, I wouldn't be hurting him any."

"No. Maybe not. But he's responsible for those saws. And if you took one in the way you planned to, he would have a hard time explaining what became of it. As a matter of fact he would be accused of aiding you. Of course if you succeeded in getting away he would have to take his punishment without the possibility of getting revenge on you for doing this dirty trick on him. But if you didn't get away I'm afraid it would be too bad for you."

"I could tell them I stole the saw."

"They wouldn't believe it. And even if they were inclined to give the machinist the benefit of the doubt set up in your confession, he would have lost his job, although he escaped the other punishment. They would not trust a man in his job to whom the slightest suspicion can be attached."

Frank pursued his plans no further. While his plot appeared to him free of violence in so far as its execution was concerned, he had failed to see the violence inherent in its results. Even though he had successfully escaped, the machinist, innocent though he was, would have had to pay bitter for his success.

Personally I cannot believe that any success gained at the misfortune of another, can have a permanent value. For many years I tried to make violence pay: but always violence made me pay.

It is true that men appear to succeed at the expense of their fellowmen. Whether or not that success gives them the pleasure it is thought to give there, is another question. One thing is certain, there is no spiritual gratification possible where violence enters in. And, speaking from my own experience, if there is any pleasure in life where moral and spiritual gratification is absent I have failed to find it.

During the past six years I've gained a spiritual inch or so. I would not barter that inch for all the gold, all the fame, and all the worldly honor in existence. I've had gold, quantities of it, crooked gold, and I've paid in a million different ways for every tainted ounce of it.

*   *   *   *   *

One of the penalties of success achieved by violence is that it must be constantly guarded by violence. It was no pleasure for me to ride in a high-priced car and be always on the alert for a spattering of machine-gun bullets from the guns of my rivals in crime. When you so live that in every man you see an enemy, there is small feeling of security in the touch of a pistol at your side. You may put a pistol under your pillow at night, but the action proves of little value in the way of inducing sleep. Nor may it give you much satisfaction to know that every penitentiary is waiting to receive you; that every electric chair has a claim on your patronage; that every noose hangs in readiness to twine itself round your neck.

I have found nothing more lastingly pleasurable than that which I possess today. I have nothing that selfish greed might envy. Therefore I need no gun to protect it. After an honest day's work, I can sit down in my home and with my family round me enjoy the quiet simple life of mutual love and spiritual harmony. If some one drops in, and this frequently occurs, bearing with him or her the weight of a troubled heart, we look upon such a visitor, not as an unwelcome guest, but as welcome opportunity to serve the one cause in the world that gives permanent gratification. In the atmosphere of our home, troubles and worries are soon dissolved, clear thinking re-established, and those who seek us with their problems usually leave with those problems solved. We preach to no one; but we have a philosophy that is creative, and in that philosophy there is no room for fear and worry. We try to make people see that fear and worry are not always constructive; that these qualities create problems and troubles; that love and clear thinking turn problems into experiences, and experiences into the gold of knowledge; that where there is knowledge there is security, and where there is security there is livingness in its highest sense of satisfaction.

And when the last symphony has died away in our radio; when our books have been put aside; when our evening meditation has been stamped upon the subjective heavens, and we have retired to our pillows, the sweetest blessing in life comes stealing over us, perfect slumber.

To be able to lie down in positive security with unlocked doors, and never turn over until another day has dawned, that is one of the gains I wouldn't exchange for all the kingdoms that have been built upon the leaping flames of violence.

There are two forms of violence, the passive and the active. Both are destructive, but not in the same degree. While active violence invariably reaches out to destroy other people and things, the passive form remains at home to destroy the person alone who harbors it. Of the two forms the latter is the most deadly to its subject, because it finds no relief in action or active expression, but remains suppressed within the individual, poisoning his nervous system, unbalancing his emotional life, arresting his powers of rational thought—all of which set up dangerous reflexes in his physical organism, which often result in grave nervous and mental disorders, while these in turn condition the body for numerous diseases, both real and hysterical, which very frequently prove fatal.

The unfortunate victim of passive violence is a physical, moral and mental coward. His cowardice furnishes the driving motive for his cruel instincts. He seeks escape from the condemnation his own mind tortures him with through the vicarious method of imagination. Deploring his own weakness, he envies the courage in others. He lacks the intestinal stamina to kill an insect, but in his imagination he visualizes himself ruthlessly crushing every one who opposes the things he would like to do. He is a killer who never kills; he is a tyrant whose tyranny touches no one but himself. He is a pathetic creature in a world that offers him no honor, no self respect, no social adjustment, no privilege of advancement.

The prisons are full of such victims. They are usually confined for moral crimes, because they lack necessary courage to commit crimes that involve physical danger. And since the nature of their crimes is such as it is, they are detested by their fellows; because, strange as it may seem, one criminal will appear to sicken at a certain type of crime committed by another.

These victims, however, are quickly responsive to love and understanding. Because of this I was able to help a few toward a more mature emotional life.

*   *   *   *   *

The case of Emmett Edwards comes speedily to mind. Emmett knew but one penalty to mete out to those with whom he disagreed. They should be shot, or hanged, or broken on some medieval instrument of torture. He was the shyest person I've ever seen and the most colossal coward.

If the fellow with whom he happened to be celling made life miserable for him, he endured the condition rather than face the deputy warden with a request for a change of cells. He simply could not screw up enough courage to face an official. And when he could not avoid such a calamity, the ordeal would leave him limp for a week to follow. He shrank from the boisterous crudeness of his comrades. He was afraid of crowds. He always agreed verbally for fear of being drawn into an argument. He shrank from entering the general shower-bath; or of being exposed to a medical examination; or to the examination conducted in the prison bureau of criminal identification. He feared the possibility of being reported for violating prison rules, or of being called upon to perform some task exposing him to the scrutiny and possible criticism of others. He feared both life and death. And he sought escape from all his fears by nursing a secret violence against anything and everything. Although this false escape channel was sufficient in itself to destroy him in time, when he added physical self abuse to it he was in possession of an annihilating combination that would be satisfied with nothing short of complete wreckage.

At the time I singled him out for laboratory experimentation, his face was drawn and sallow, his eyes were hollow with black circles round them. The skin on his neck had begun to crease, it was thick and oily. His head was becoming pinched at the temples, the brow was tightening, his lips were drawing back from his teeth, giving his features the appearance of an eternal grin, or silly grimace. His hands had a sickly yellowish color, and the nails had the bloodless blue of heavy or sluggish circulation. He was emaciated and his mind was already touched by feebleness.

Summing him up briefly, I classified him, first, as a victim of passive violence, and second, as a victim of both passive and active violence, the latter being aimed at himself. At first I scarcely knew which one of these types of violence to attack first.

Dad Trueblood suggested that the elimination of

the one would have a strong tendency to eliminate the other along with it. Obviously, however, the violence he was expressing actively against himself as the most urgent consideration, since it was doing the greatest amount of physical and mental harm at the moment.

Emmett had reached the place on his march to destruction where the line between sanity and insanity is very thin. One of the peculiar features of these borderline cases is that they become super-sensitive at this point to an almost unbelievable degree. They can tell in an instant whether they are being watched covertly, and thoughts, especially if they are adverse, directed toward them are picked up with the ease and accuracy of a radio receiving set.

For about a week I treated Emmett silently with the constructive thoughts of love. At first he showed every indication of being greatly disturbed by them. He would fidget and strive to locate their source by trying to catch their sender in the act of looking at him. His reaction to the influence was different. That much he could feel. He had become more or less inured to the critical thoughts his fellows had been holding for him; but these thoughts of love—there was something foreign about them that sent him to reacting involuntarily in a most uncomfortable way.

By and by, however, the influence of love acting upon creative principle, began to have the desired effect, that of soothing and calming its object. He came to recognize this influence as being pleasant. He could sense that others had the power to disturb it when they came near him to speak, and he resented this, and would avoid it whenever possible. But when I finally approached him to carry out my campaign of suggestion, he found that I did not disturb him; that instead of feeling a sense of repulsion he experienced a feeling of attraction. And this was the ground work I had been wanting to lay.

In this boy's case and my connection with it, I learned what friendship is and what a friend really means to one who all his life had starved for the things only a friend has power to give. A friend, I discovered, is one with whom you can share yourself completely: your secrets, your sins, your weaknesses, your hopes and disappointments—all your faults, your failures and your triumphs. A friend is one with whom you can be the real you. A friend is one in whom you can place the last full measure of trust and know it will never be misplaced.

To Emmett I became that sort of friend. There wasn't a secret that he didn't divulge to me. He took me back into his childhood, and there he described for me one incident that gave me the cause for his life of cowardly misery.

It happened on his first day at school and his first encounter with that species of cruelty that only school children can inflict upon their fellows. Emmett had been challenged to do battle, and although he gamely accepted the challenge and for a while annoyed his larger opponent, the conflict grew too warm for him and he "hollered nuff" from his underneath position on the battleground.

The ridicule that followed branded him forever as a coward. He was never allowed to hear the end of it. He heard it from his own brothers and sisters and even his father, and he finally came to accept it as an inevitable part of him.

Since the cause of cowardice in his case had been the result of physical defeat, I promptly concluded that the reconditioning process should begin by establishing a sense of physical courage, while at the same time stimulating a desire in his mind for and pride in the possibilities of his body.

To this end I made arrangements for a magazine that dealt with physical culture. Then I began mild scuffing matches with him. These developed into boxing matches. And finally I induced him to don the gloves with me before an enthusiastic circle of fans.

By permitting him to give me a pretty rough pummelling on this occasion, his self confidence rose to egotistical heights, and every day thereafter I found myself being invited to do a few rounds, which I of course accepted, but not always to his advantage. He proved to me, however, that he could take it on the chin and bore right in for more.

In three months' time his interest in things athletic had become a passion. He came to admire his physique. And then one day the best boxer in the shop challenged him, he accepted, and gave the fellow one of the worst maulings he had ever had in his life.

With this accomplishment he had that respect physical inferiority always pays to physical superiority. And, having been a coward, his courage now was genuine, not of the false bully type that finds sadistic pleasure in preying on weakness, but the kind that defends weakness. He was later to organize the baseball team of our shop, and still later to become the captain of the first team, and still later Emmett Edwards became the director of all prison athletics, and was one of the first contestants to enter a real prison prize ring, a Fourth of July feature created by his efforts, while three thousand spectators looked on and rooted for their respective favorite on whom they had laid their bets of tobacco and other items of prison luxury.

From a craven coward and physical wreck, Emmett

had climbed to the peak of courage in one year's time. A mighty gap to span, but not a difficult one when love and creative law worked hand in hand behind the gap-jumper to bring the feat about.

*   *   *   *   *

It is sometimes claimed that creative progress is faster working on the down-grade than it is on the up-grade. But the little experience I have had disproves this theory.

The example just recounted, for instance, shows beyond doubt that when the creative principle is reversed from destruction to construction, the destructive achievement that required years to attain was equaled if not surpassed in the period of only one year, when its final measure had been attained in the opposite direction.

And again in my own case, in a period of only a few months I was able to sublimate habits that had taken twenty years to build into my life. Indeed, as I have also pointed out, in cases of disease with a hysterical background of long standing, the creative cure was brought about almost instantly once the cause for destructive creation was isolated and the creative law set to work in the constructive direction of health.

But after all, it is the arguing about definitions and theories that creates the confusion so prevalent today, and that results in so much limitation on the part of those who need the application of creative principle far more than they need the learned expositions of what that principle is, how it works, and what it is calculated to do. *Actually and really, the only thing one needs to know about any law, or principle, is that it exists, that it can be used for either good or bad, according to the love or desire motive of the indi-*

vidual, and that it always works, in the one direction or the other.

To waste valuable time quibbling about definitions and theories while all the time need pleads for application, is, in my humble opinion, the summed-up total of all that is unintelligent, unpractical, and certainly unproductive.

If a person suffering from illness went to a doctor and the doctor, instead of applying medical treatment, defined the science of medicine, told how it worked, and what it was calculated to achieve, such a patient would be no better off after leaving the doctor than he was before seeing him.

Application is the final test of any law, and to make that application it is not necessary to subject the law, an infallible principle, to the analysis of a fallible human mind.

CHAPTER 6
Love and the Prison Door of Death

Dust, to its narrow house beneath!
Soul to its place on high!
They that have seen thy face in death,
No more may fear to die.
— *Mrs. Hemans.*

Does the continuity of the life-chain remain unbroken at death? Whilst it is instinctive and reasonable to believe in immortality, to many people, belief without supporting proof is like faith that produces only the vague realization of its evidence. Where realization is incomplete there is no sense of certainty; and where there is no sense of certainty, satisfaction is only partially experienced; and where satisfaction is only partially experienced, troublesome doubts haunt the mind with annoying fears, and thus a life that was created with inherent capacities of security becomes insecure and miserable.

Most people fear death in one degree or another. They approach it, not inwardly courageous, but with a sort of dull fatalistic emotion; their fear of it being made bearable by the fact that it is inescapable and that every one must face it alike sooner or later. This is one of the many curious graces of life, of compensation, that dread loses much of its sting when shared by others.

But can immortality be proven to the intellect in the same manner in which a scientist might prove the existence of a natural law? Yes and no. A scientist working with concrete facts before him may arrive at his law and prove it by the facts assembled. For instance, Newton, observing the fall of an apple, began to wonder why it didn't fall up instead of down. From the observation of this fact, he began his investigations that later brought him to his law of gravitation. To prove this law we have only to toss an object in the air and watch it being drawn back to earth. With immortality, however, the procedure is somewhat different. The fact of death occurs, but contemporary men who pass on fail to return in such a manner as to make their testimony of the hereafter valid and acceptable.

With this problem one may experiment only with one's self. And while one may prove to one's self intellectually that the life-chain remains unbroken at death, one may not prove this truth to another, because the concrete evidence, the body, once the life-force has been withdrawn from it, offers no proof of anything, save that death has occurred. As the light-bulb refuses to reveal where the light goes when the switch is pressed, so does the cold body refuse to reveal where the life-force goes when the mortal heart has ceased to function.

Reason may give another convincing testimony of survival, but not tangible proof. Take the monumental testimony of Sir Thomas Browne, for example. "There is nothing strictly immortal," said he, "but immortality. Whatever has no beginning may be confident to have no end." That is sound reason based upon scientific deduction, because even the most materialistic mind cannot conceive a beginning of life. And certainly to presume an end for something that had no beginning is, at best, to presume an impossibility. But while convincing reason may give courage by strengthening faith, it can prove nothing to the intellect of another. It may remove the greater part of death's sting; but it will not remove the gigantic question mark. That must be accomplished in the laboratory of one's own mind.

There is a way to go about it. A scientific way. I am not the discoverer of this way by any means. Eastern seers have been employing the method for centuries, perhaps. I did, however, get an original realization of the method's existence some time before I saw it formulated in specific detail. And while I may describe the method to you, I can prove nothing to your intellect, unless you evoke enough interest to apply the method, in which case you will inevitably arrive at your own proof, the only possible way to arrive at proof on this most important question.

*   *   *   *   *

By this time it had been noised about the prison that since I had entered the cell of Dad Trueblood I had learned from him the art of getting along with almost everybody, no matter how disagreeable the person was with others. I was not surprised, therefore, and neither was Dad, when one day the warden sent for me and offered me a job in the prison hospital. I found the doctor in the warden's office when I arrived there. The warden asked me bluntly if I was afraid of death or contagion.

I was able to answer promptly and sincerely, "No, I have no fear of the one nor faith in the other."

He looked at me quizzically for a moment. Then he asked, "Do you mean you don't believe in death?"

"I believe there is a transition called death," I replied. "In fact, I know there is. But I have neither fear, faith, nor belief in death as a door that cannot be opened with love and understanding before it is reached in the natural way."

"Have you proven this to your satisfaction?" he asked.

"Only upon the evidence of reason, warden. It is my hope to prove it by experience some day without having to wait for the experience of death itself."

Both the warden and the doctor had evidently pondered deeply on the subject, but both had come to about the same conclusion. They saw in death a scientific fact of life. Beyond that whatever speculations they had entertained had dissipated into a sort of nebulous agnosticism.

I put the question to them both. "Do you believe there is a power higher than that expressed through the brain of man?"

The doctor's ready answer surprised me, for it was sharply metaphysical and strangely illuminating for a purely medical minded man. He said he knew there was a power operating in the universe beside which man's brain was comparatively nothing. "But," he qualified, "I believe there's a latent capacity in the brain of man that, if it could be fully utilized, would include all the power existent, both natural and supernatural."

"You've expressed it better than I could, doctor," I told him. And then the warden told me of a condition in the hospital I already knew about, since it was a common topic throughout the prison.

In the tuberculosis ward was a patient known quite aptly as Poison Jasper. This man was about to wind up a long and arduous career of crime. He was ending it, however, true to his colors. Whatever else could be said of him, he determined to die as he had lived, ferociously, consistent to the end.

For months he had been wasting away. As a patient he was the most ungovernable in the ward. As a man his heart was as bitter and black as any heart could be. His fellow patients feared him. He would laugh and sneer at his dying comrades who sought solace in a last prayer or who called for the prison chaplain in their final hour. He picked arguments with those round him. The doctor avoided the caustic in his tongue whenever he could do so. And the warders were made constant objects of his vile abuse. There was, of course, no way to discipline the man, since the state law forbade the infliction of punishment on the sick and dying.

When he could not rail and rant at men, he cursed the God in whom he had never believed. He was a fanatical disbeliever and was proud to declare it at any moment the occasion might present itself. Nurse after nurse had been driven from the hospital by his fiendish attacks upon them. Every one about him wished and longed for the day of his demise, a fact which he knew all too well, and which he answered with a tightening of his will to live on in spite of their wishes. One of his most demonic traits would spring to the surface when some dying patient would send for the chaplain and the latter, because of some one of many possible reasons, would fail to comply. The reason, of course, would be conveyed to the patient.

But Poison Jasper would always scoff at such excuses, as he called them. "The same old alibi," he would cackle throatily, "a preacher, a man of God, afraid to stick his nose in this ward for fear he'll breathe one of our germs. He can tell all you human skeletons how to die, all about heaven, what a swell joint it is. But he'd just as soon stay right here. He's yellow. He's a rank coward."

These tirades were palpably unjust; yet he sincerely

believed them to be true. He detested any one who evinced fear of the disease that was gradually rubbing out his own life.

Before I accepted the task, taming Poison Jasper, I talked to Dad Trueblood about it.

"Well, it ain't that I want to lose a good cell-buddy," he said. "But I don't aim to meddle in your destiny. Every experience presented to us holds something for us, if we'll only open our eyes and try to find it. Go on up and do your best for them poor devils. You can't lose anything, and you might gain a lot."

Old Dad Trueblood possessed an authentic sense of prophecy that I had learned by this time to heed. I expressed doubt, however, as to my ability to handle the situation.

"Lissen," Dad said thoughtfully, "Old Jasper's just a poor misguided and misunderstood child. *Put love in your eye for him, and then make him look at it. You'll probably be surprised at the result.*"

In the event I found it hard to evoke that love and he explained how I might accomplish it. But first he quoted a passage from Young:

"Men drop so fast, ere life's mid stage we tread,
Few know so many friends alive as dead."

"Those who now hate Old Jasper most," he went on, "will be unable to hold that hate when they look upon his still features. In the presence of the dead the faults of the past are dissolved and the virtues of the past are resurrected. So just look at Old Jasper and imagine that the Almighty has closed his weary lids and forgiven all the human errors and weaknesses. In the presence of the dead the faults that once were are dissolved and the virtues that were are resurrected. So just look at Old Jasper and imagine he's no more.

The love of which I spoke will well up in you and your eyes will become its windows."

He also explained what I was later to learn in a most significant and helpful way, that tubercular patients were acutely sensitive to the opinions of others, expressed or unexpressed. That they could detect the faintest tremor of fear on the part of the nurse, and this they resented, because it weakened the hope they desired to retain to the end. If the nurse was afraid of their disease, what hope had they of becoming cured?

"Too," Dad added, "some of the cases will have a purely imaginary basis. If your actions are fearless and your hints to them convincing and constructive, you might succeed in supplanting the sick thought in their minds with a well thought strong enough to set their minds to building new bodily tissue faster than the germs can destroy it. With this, hope will likewise become stronger; faith will increase; the will to survive will take on renewed persistence; bodily resistance will grow in proportion; and as the power of resistance increases the destructive power of the germs will decrease. T.B. germs don't thrive on resistance, but on a lack of it."

*   *   *   *   *

When I walked into the ward the next night, I was immediately conscious of the strained, fearful and suspicious atmosphere of the place. With me I had brought an old copy of Volney's "Ruins of Empire." Dad had told me to give it to Jasper, and to tell him casually that one of his old cronies had asked me to bring it in to him. I was to mention also, that he must keep the book hidden when the keeper was around; that it was a book on the chaplain's restriction list; and that if it was discovered that I had brought it to him, I would be thrown into the dungeon for breaking this rule.

Jasper mumbled something in a grudging tone about his not being the kind of a rat who would knife a man who favored him. I had nothing to fear on that score. But he was obviously suspicious of me as he had been of all the other nurses who had preceded me. I could plainly see that he was determined not to show any signs of friendliness toward me. But the book incident had disarmed him and he was forced, unwillingly of course, at least to respect a man who would gamble with the dungeon in order to do him, a total stranger, a good turn.

For several nights I was aware that Jasper watched me like an evil cat waiting for a justifiable opportunity to pounce upon its prey. It was a game of wits I played with him. I parried with all the skill I had at my command to forestall the opening he sought. My second victory over him was scored on the night my first patient passed on.

The dying man had begged for the chaplain to come over and administer last minute prayers and spiritual consolation. But, unfortunately, the chaplain was away from the prison at the time. Knowing what Jasper would have to say when this disheartening news came back, I had prepared for the event. I had taken up a position at the foot of Jasper's bed, and was standing there looking down at him when the keeper came with the message—I was looking down at him and reasoning in my heart that I stood before a potential Christ. In fact, I knew I was standing before a potential Christ. The only difference was that Christ had used the medium of love to create a useful life, while Jasper had used it to create a misspent life. Plainly, under such circumstances of reasoning, Jasper, not being so fortunate as Christ, deserved sympathy instead of censure, love instead of hate. This feeling consumed me as I stood there. Just as the keeper informed the dying patient that the chaplain was away at the time, Jasper looked me squarely in the eye, opened his mouth to unlimber a bitter epithet, then turned his eyes from mine without speaking.

"I've never said many prayers," I told him in a confidential tone, "but I've a notion to try it for that poor guy. If doing that much will make things seem a little easier for him, I believe I'd feel pretty much like a cad not to do it. What do you think, Jasper?"

He made no comment. But he studied me intently as I lifted the patient in my arms and asked him to follow my words in his mind. The man died in this position, apparently comforted by the awkward but sincere prayer of a layman. His head had dropped against my shoulder, somewhat in the manner of a tired babe falling to sleep.

It was this test of my disregard for the disease that convinced Jasper I had no fear of it. It also convinced all my other patients, and because of this incident the morale of the patients was lifted to a marked degree.

From that moment on until Jasper's hour to go had arrived, there was no more trouble with him during my time on duty. In the day-time, however, he made no such voluntary concessions as he had reluctantly conceded to me.

*   *   *   *   *

Jasper died about two o'clock one morning. He died without any apparent fear or pain. His mind was active and he was able to whisper right up to the last minute. Yet he had asked for no spiritual consolation, and he indicated no complaint.

Ten minutes before the end came his body began to relax. The hard brutal lines on his wasted face softened, and the eyes that had burned so feverishly and fiercely in their sunken black sockets, became softly brilliant, like a pair of luminous twin stars. Standing directly in front of him, I seemed unable to hold his gaze. While his eyes were fastened directly on me, they appeared to be fastened on something through and far beyond me. He beckoned feebly and I sat down on the edge of his bed.

"I'm dying," he whispered.

Of course I knew he spoke the truth, but I awkwardly sought to reassure him.

"Don't be a fool," he murmured. "I see it all there as plain as day."

"Where? What?" I asked, leaning eagerly toward his lips for the answer.

"I tell you I'm dying," he repeated, ignoring my query. "I tell you I can see——" His eyes rolled upward and the lids partly closed over them.

This incident I put down as a deathbed visual hallucination, and allowed it to pass quickly from my thoughts. Then several days later, during my sleep period, I was awakened out of a dream that had to do with this patient. It seemed that I had failed in my effort to draw the lids over his eyes. I dozed off again and immediately I began dreaming of the garden and the Christ Who walked there. This time the words were first in my mind when again I had awakened. One phrase was, "Lift up thine eyes to Heaven," and the other, "Let thine eye be single."

The dream itself seemed to have no special significance; nor was it unusual. Doubtless many persons have had similar dreams. It was the channel of thought it opened up that stirred me so profoundly. An observation I had made numerous times before became sharply provocative.

Why was it, I thought, that during the transition from life to death the eyeballs turned upward instead of downward?

I began to probe into the question in search of a reasonable answer. Certainly the action was contrary to nature. The well-trained muscles that controlled the movement of the eyeballs were adjusted to only two natural positions, the level position, and the downward position. Rolling the eyeballs up was neither natural nor an easy feat to accomplish even by force. It seemed quite singular, therefore, that in death the eyeballs would ignore natural custom and roll up instead of down, thus making an exception to a life-long rule of following the habit of least resistance. That death brought muscular relaxation failed, as it seemed to me, to account for the phenomenon.

Later, as I continued to ponder the matter, I came into possession of a fugitive piece of reading material. And this in itself was strange, although such relative things do seem to have a peculiar way, often a most curious way, of finding those in search of that particular type of information sought.

In this paper the author told how when the eyes were down as in ordinary sleep, we drifted through dream states evolved from the subconscious reservoir of memory. When the eyes were level, as in our waking hours, we were living in the conscious state of being. When the eyeballs were lifted upward in meditation, we entered into the metaphysical realm. The paper, also, gave a detailed system for practice which I promptly began to follow.

My practice was carried on in a darkened room while I lay flat on my back without pillows. It took me many days so to train the unaccustomed muscles that controlled the movement of the eyeballs before I could make them respond to my wishes easily and free of strain, that is, before I could lift my eyeballs and hold them in that position without their tiring or becoming fluttery.

When I had accomplished this a most surprising thing happened. I sat down one night to snatch a brief period of meditation. Closing my eyes, I began to think about the many things that had come to me of late for which to feel grateful. As I continued to enumerate them silently, I felt an irresistible tugging sensation in my eyes, and presently, without conscious effort on my part, I was aware that my eyeballs were being drawn upward toward a single focal point in the center of my forehead. On this point they became riveted. *As they did so, the effect was that of turning on an electric switch. The entire front part of my head became illuminated with brilliant multicolored light. In comparison the light of the sun was as a white beam beside a radium dial; a candle beside a lighthouse beacon.*

To me the discovery was a sublime revelation. I became immersed in the boundless luminosity of it. The consciousness of self vanished in it. I no longer appeared as an individualized speck in the universal scheme of things. I was the universe itself, with all its limitless freedom, its endless expansion, its blissful enchantment. A mighty symphony of celestial music seemed to vibrate through my uncurbed being. I saw and heard what Poison Jasper saw and heard when he told me not to be a fool, that he saw it all as plain as day. I saw more, I saw my own body, inert, motionless, apparently lifeless, and I had compassion on those who were compelled to live in such cramped quarters as the body I had inhabited, and now looked upon from a perspective vantage point of limitless freedom and joy.

By and by the luminosity began to gather into a unity of one color, a mauve purple, and out of this there presently appeared at the spot where my eyes were riveted, a perfectly pointed star. It presented the illusion of vast distance, although though it appeared quite near. When I opened my eyes, the warder was shaking my arm and informing me that a patient was in need of attention. He thought I had fallen asleep. But I hadn't. I had never been so much awake. In that brief moment I had proven to my intellect that I possessed an immortal soul. In that short period of time, I received the secret in the Master's words uttered to me in a dream. I knew what He meant when He said "Lift up thine eyes to Heaven." I knew in that star between my eyes I had found the eye that is forever single.

I've died twice daily and once nightly since that first discovery. Three times during the twenty-four hours I induce the little death in exchange for a few moments of the boundless life.

As I plainly stated at the beginning of this chapter, immortality can be proven to the intellect in a scientific way and by a scientific method. But I cannot, nor can any one else, prove it to the intellect of another. I say again, it is not my desire to prove, but to describe. To those of you, however, who have feared death, and who have doubted the unbroken continuity of life, I can assure you that a little effort will give to you the proof that it gave to me; and perhaps at a much less expenditure of effort for I, like Poison Jasper, can hardly be considered a person with unusual psychic development. I'm not. I've lived a hard doubting, skeptical life. Even now I come from metaphysical meditations doubting many of the very things I've realized there. Had I been more sensitive to the cosmic influences than I am, my spiritual conflict would have been over with the discovery just recounted. But the human animal is still very much alive in me, and I have still many arresting habits that must be sublimated before the smoke of Armageddon's war ceases to roll in blotting clouds across my mind.

But if you need more than the evidence of faith, if you are one of those persons who are compelled by nature to find our way by reason and experiment, as I am; if you need intellectual proof, if you must realize immortality through actual experience here and now, if you really care to contact the fourth dimension by a conscious method and explore for yourself the vast realm of superconsciousness—I repeat, if you are sincerely interested, enough so to make the little effort necessary, then you need search no farther for the means to that end. It is in your hands. You have only to use it. No information is worth an iota to the person who merely receives it and does not apply it.

*   *   *   *   *

This chapter has been read in manuscript by several persons of varying faiths and schools of thought, including one occultist and an orthodox minister. By the latter I was informed that no one should dare to experiment in this manner, that one should not deliberately meddle in destiny.

Not in another person's destiny, perhaps, but in your own destiny—by all means.

The occultist informed me in the most vibrant tones that I had stumbled upon a secret that had been known to Eastern seers for centuries. I didn't stumble upon it. It was attracted to me when I was ready to use it. One of the very seers he mentioned authored the paper that came into my hands and gave me the method I later used successfully. The same seer is today busy trying to give the method to others.

Another bit of information my occultist critic gave me was, "You should guard this wisdom lest it fall into the hands of others—others who in their ignorance or avarice might misuse it."

Now of course I'm no seer nor adept. I've lived no life of renunciation or strict austerity. I've just blundered along through life like fate, taking the hard knocks that invariably accompany unintelligent living, and finally after a long time awaking up to the fact that there was such a thing as plain mule sense in the world for any one who wanted to use it.

This mule sense tells me, despite the warning of my occult friend, that neither knowledge nor wisdom can be misused. To have wisdom is to have a realization of truth, and to have a realization, a consciousness of truth, is to be uplifted by it. In my humble opinion, the capacity to receive truth is God's guarantee against its misuse; and surely any guarantee of God's is man's opportunity to rise, not sink.

I was reminded, likewise, that one should knock at the door of higher levels of understanding inspired only by the highest motives, thus revealing to me that he had never remotely approached true superconscious being. The methods employed to open this door are of no importance whatever, save as a means to an end. The motive may be the worst form of selfishness, an idle sense of curiosity. The important thing is to open the door. Once opened, and during the stay therein, human motives vanish, all low human qualities and characteristics become wholly and completely dissolved in the illimitable sea of all-pervading truth.

Immerged in this sea all meditation becomes impersonal; the finite aspect of love falls away as universal love closes in around you. You think without being conscious of thinking, you feel without being conscious of feeling, you receive all without appearing to receive. Always you come out of these meditations a better spiritual entity than when you entered.

And since the ultimate purpose of life is to grow spiritually, I disagree with those who would tell you not to meddle in your own destiny and not approach the door that leads to life eternal.

CHAPTER 7
Love and the Prison Door of Disease

All bodily disease which we look upon as whole and entire within itself, may after all, be but a symptom of some ailment in the spiritual past.
—Hawthorne.

If this chapter might later appear to have been misnamed, I can assure the reader that such is not the case. Love operating through me made it possible to break down natural human restraints, obtain confidence in the cases described, and thus get to the real causes that were responsible for the diseases manifest.

My experiences in the prison hospital included many of such cases. Most of them I was able to cure without the use of drugs. Some I failed to cure, because the conditioning habit of morbidity had become so deeply rooted in the subconscious life of the patient that my inventive resources failed to uncover an effective means of treatment.

Before I get farther into the chapter, I wish to make it understood now that in neither of the first two cases mentioned here was there an organic basis for the diseases treated. In each case the underlying cause was mental. During this time and since, I've treated and cured scores of sick and crippled people of every conceivable kind and degree of affliction. And in every case where I was able to effect a cure the manifestation of affliction was hysterical and not organic. I have never been able to effect a cure in purely

121

organic cases. I do not, however, wish to infer that such cures cannot be accomplished by others; but that they haven't been accomplished by me, and certainly in making this statement a great mistake would be made by any one accepting it as a general rule rather than a particular one. I can and do, nevertheless, offer it as my belief that at least half of the sickness in America, especially, is due to unwholesome mental habits, such as destructive suggestibility. The following case will illustrate clearly what I mean.

The man in question was highly intelligent, very sensitive, and extremely cocksure about his own opinions.

He was carried into the hospital late one night suffering from extreme pain in the abdomen. He said to me as I helped him remove his clothing, "I know what's the matter with me. But don't say anything. I want to see if the doctor knows."

When the doctor reached him and made his examination, he diagnosed the pain as gall colic. "You're absolutely right, doctor," the patient said, "I'm lousy with gall-stones." He manifested every possible symptom of this disease.

Since the case seemed to call for an immediate operation, the surgeon was called from his bed. He reached the prison hospital in no pleasant frame of mind. He examined the patient carefully, and later announced that the fellow was suffering from the effects of an exaggerated imagination; that what he needed was a metaphysical practitioner instead of a surgeon.

"Still," he added, "if you can't find any other way to reach him, we may have to operate as a gesture in order to save his life. If he gets any worse by morning give me a ring."

"See what you can do," the hospital physician said to me, and I started on the trail of the mental quirk that had brought the fellow's trouble about.

In the first place the man was suffering severe pain, and to this I responded with a wholehearted sympathy. I made an effort to do what I could, in a physical way, for him, while at the same time I was planning how best I might approach him in my effort to help him in a mental way.

By careful and tactful leads I succeeded in getting him to talk about himself and his opinions between grunts and groans. I assumed the role of a poorly informed but sympathetic listener, eager to profit by the sage advice I well knew he was capable of giving me. Thus he revealed in due time that he had been an inveterate reader of newspaper health articles.

He was that type of susceptible person to whom health information was quite as likely as not to prove a liability instead of an asset. Indeed to one of these articles he had unwittingly fallen prey. The article had been written by a famous doctor on the subject of gall-stones.

At the time he read the article there was a slight but annoying muscular pain in the abdominal region where gall-colic occurs. The pain appeared to him to be identical with that described by the writer. So he promptly grew alarmed and began to diagnose his own case, which was of course gall-stones. And by the time he reached the hospital all the symptoms of this disease were rejected in his physical organism.

Now that I had the cause, it became a complicated problem as to how I might eradicate it. Obviously I could not do it by the use of reason or suggestion. By making myself a pupil of his, as it were, I had destroyed the opportunity to make a sudden right-about face and become his teacher. Besides, he was entirely too opinionated to be convinced against his will. There was nothing to do, therefore, but let him cure himself, while I did the directing, although I appeared not to be doing so.

As I pondered on a method, a brilliant idea occurred to me. In my room was a book written by a doctor who advocated fasting in the cure and prevention of disease. Later in the morning, I paused at his door to inquire after him, and I had the book in my hand. He asked me the title of it. I told him, and mentioned casually that I had just been reading the chapter on gall-stones. As I expected he asked to see it. I gave him the book, and went on about my duties. When again I had returned his eyes were burning with enthusiasm.

"Here's a doctor that knows his business," he said. "If I could get the treatment prescribed here I could cure myself."

"Well," I replied, "they don't allow any unortho- dox treatment here in the hospital. But I'm willing to trust you and take a chance." This statement pleased him. "You tell me what to do," I added, "and I'll follow instructions."

Thus it was, I took four ounces of olive oil and four ounces of orange juice, whipped them together, and gave it to him at six that morning. During the day he refused food. At seven that night, when I came on duty again, he instructed me to give him a high warm enema, which I did. As I well knew it would, this brought away a great quantity of hard green pellets of bile. We secured seventy-seven of these small pellets in all. Immediately following this demonstration, every symptom of gall-stone left the man. He remained in the hospital, however, for six more days fasting on orange juice according to the advice given in the book. Then he pronounced himself cured and returned to his cell. Until I left the prison this fellow carried a dozen or so of these bile pellets around in a match box and never passed up an opportunity to display them to any one who was curious to know just what a gall-stone really looked like.

In this instance I might also add, that the case described above was only one of several encountered during my hospital experience whose causes were traced back to the reading of health articles, medical books, patent medicine circulars and the like.

Several years ago the press conducted a vigorous educational campaign against cancer. As a direct result of reading these informational articles and editorials, two prisoners developed typical symptoms of stomach cancer, one of which died a lingering painful death, and the other I treated and cured by convincing him I possessed curative powers in my hands, which I placed over the affected regions and advised him to feel the flow of curative magnetism pouring from my hands to the cancerous growth. His own belief, or if you'd rather, his own faith in the mastery of my apparent power, did the work by replacing in his mind a well thought instead of the sick one he had been entertaining.

*   *   *   *   *

Before taking up case number two I wish to take issue with many people who deplore the use of deception in any form or for any reason. In nearly all mental treatments, deceptions, ruses of some kind, must be resorted to in order to get the cause of the trouble and apply an effective counteractant. The creative principle does not recognize the right or wrong of anything. But the use that man makes of a thing determines its moral quality. Any vice may be turned into a virtue by reversing its trend and setting it in motion toward the ends of virtue.

Case number two was undoubtedly the most amazing example I've ever seen or heard about in the realm of hysterically induced physical disabilities. He was an absolute wreck. He was brought from the court room to the prison on a stretcher to begin an indeterminate sentence. It had been predicted at the time that he would cheat the law of its prey long before the board of paroles had a chance to act on his case.

His hospital chart revealed him a sufferer of paralysis of limbs, hardening of the liver, diabetes, dropsy tendencies, arthritis, tuberculosis of the bowels, heart-leakage, neuroticism, faulty-vision and high blood pressure.

So the reader might, also, share the assumption of the time that this man was in a dying condition. Because of its relative importance, I wish to add one item that was not listed on the chart. The fellow was an illiterate and was childishly superstitious, as I soon discovered.

At the time he committed the crime, a shooting affair, for which he had been convicted, he had been in apparent good health.

It took me several nights to break through the wall of secrecy he had built up around himself. Suspicious and slow to trust, he was chary of strangers; he was on guard against anything that seemed like an approach to his inner life. I didn't press him, but I did evoke a strong feeling of love for him, and I missed no opportunity to express that love in tangible terms that he could not only feel but understand. Inch by inch the bars went down. Then one night he made a confession with all the naiveté of a child.

In the neighborhood where he had lived all his life was an old woman who possessed strange powers of divination. She had visited him at the jail and revealed to him that he was in the clutches of The Evil One. A curse had been placed on him and a spell cast that would destroy him in a terrible way. The hands that held the gun would turn to stone, the eyes that sighted down the gun barrel would become blind, his legs would become useless, his innards like a nest of poison serpents.

Accepting this upon the infallible authority of the old woman, he promptly set his mind to the task of reflecting it all in his body. Obviously, there was but one thing to be done in his case and that was to destroy the influence of The Evil One. As in nearly all such cases it was a matter of fighting the devil, with his own weapons. Logic, reason, persuasion were puny implements compared to the implements of that devil in his determination to make the sinister curse effective. Deception had brought the man's condition about; deception would have to be resorted to in order to counteract the results of the original deception. Between two evils there is but one choice for the practitioner, the evil that can be twisted and set to work along constructive lines.

I took the doctor into my plans and obtained his permission to allow Dad Trueblood to co-operate with me. Then Dad and I worked out our campaign of attack. Since I had access to the patient's private history, and since it was I who read all his letters for him, I had in my possession a great quantity of personal information about the man, which I turned over to Dad.

Then I began to tell the patient about an old man in this very prison who had powers even greater than those possessed by the old woman he had told me about. This old man, I told him, could even tell your fortune. I could see immediately that he was interested. After awhile I suggested that he ask the doctor if he might be permitted to see the fortune-teller, and of course the doctor agreed, and sent for Dad to come over.

What a revelation it was! The patient told me afterward: "Why, he told me things no one on earth knows about but me." Time and again Dad was sent for by the patient, and with each visit the patient's faith in Dad's powers mounted higher and higher until I was able to tell Dad one day, "Well, old-timer, you've won the most exalted prize in this world, you've become a god."

"That's good," the old fellow said, "but there's much to be done. I must get absolute control of the poor devil. He's got to see me demonstrate my power over man's strongest enemy."

"You mean——?" I asked.

"Yep," he said, "he's got to see me raise the dead."

We carefully arranged for this great demonstration to take place in the room directly across the hall from the patient's room.

In this room we planted an accomplice earlier in the evening, a man presumably brought over from one of the cell-houses in a dying condition. For two or three hours there was much activity around his room, hurried darting about between many whispered consultations. The reason for all of this I conveyed in a most solemn and confidential manner to my patient across the hall who, of course, had been taking it all in. Finally, at the hour of midnight the accomplice died and I carried the tragic news over to our interested spectator.

"Listen to me," I said to him, "you stand in good

with the doctor. I want you to ask him to let Dad
Trueblood come over here and see what he can do.
The man is dead, I know; but I believe Dad can bring
him back to life."

"Do you reckon Dad could do that?"

I did. The patient told me to tell the doctor he
would like to speak with him. A few minutes later the
doctor emerged from the patient's room and winked.
And in a few more minutes the miracle man, Dad
Trueblood, was in the hospital. He didn't go directly
into the death room; but he went first into the
patient's room. Very solemnly he thanked the patient
for interceding on the dead man's behalf.

"Do you think you can really bring him back to
life?" the patient asked eagerly.

"I don't think anything about it," was Dad's reply.
"I know I can. He's not dead, but sleeping. The evil
one has cast a spell over him and a curse on him. I
am greater than The Evil One. Before my words The
Evil One flies back to the darkness where he came
from. I am The Evil Ones's master. Before me he
cannot stand. Watch!"

And the patient did watch. He watched every
gesture and heard each word that fell from Dad's lips.
He saw the dead man raise up in his bed with the
motion of Dad's hand. He saw Dad back slowly
toward the door and heard him say "Come" to the
man who a minute before had lain cold under The
Evil One's spell. And he saw the man follow Dad
into the hall and disappear down the corridor, never
again to return to the bed of death.

*And on a night a week later, the miracle man
performed the same sort of ceremony in the room of
our patient. He broke The Evil One's spell, and that
moment the hysterically produced diseases that had*

held the man in their grip for months fell away as though they had never been.

I once recounted this incident to a practicing metaphysician, a woman who had an excellent record of accomplishments to her credit. The end attained, she thought, was a worthy one; but to her the method employed was extremely revolting and sacrilegious. Had we employed the deceptions of our own invention instead of closely copying the methods of Jesus by which to perpetuate our deceptions, her criticism would have been withheld.

In my opinion, however, there is no valid parallel between our method and that of the Master. It is assumed that He was above the need of employing deceptive methods to accomplish His ends, and since we possessed no such development as this, we could not copy what we did not possess. I have no fear but that the Master, recognizing our limitations, would have readily condoned our means.

*   *   *   *   *

There is a vast difference in the attitude of a patient entering a prison hospital and one entering a hospital on outside. Such hospitals no longer hold the terror for the sick they once did, but the belief still persists among most prisoners that in the prison hospital there is a mysterious black bottle always at hand for midnight service. One dose from this bottle and there is one less convict to provide trouble for the law.

Of all the fears that harass men in prison, the worst is the fear of dying in prison. Why this should be I do not know. But there may be a touch of superstition connected with it. To a prisoner his prison represents a living hell on earth, and it might be that deep down within him he fears to die in this hell of sin and iniquity, because to do so might lessen his chances of escaping that other hell lying just across the border. Ninety-nine out of every hundred prisoners possess a psychopathic religious streak in them that comes to the surface in the form of fear when they become seriously ill.

"If I could only live long enough to get out," is the plaintive cry one hears in the prison hospitals. And it's a soul-rending cry, because of the utter hopelessness of it in most cases. It appears that in their minds is a belief that death on the outside is something of a pleasure, whilst on the inside it is something to be viewed with dread and trembling.

I stress this point here for the purpose of showing that the very desperation involved, sometimes proves the factor most needed in effecting an ultimate cure, especially in cases where the causes are organic and the affliction genuine.

The following was such a case. In it there was no mental cause to be probed for and eradicated, and yet everything depended upon establishing in the patient's mind a strong personal desire to overcome. In this instance, therefore, my duty was to discover some method whereby this desire could be planted and fostered in the patient's mind. Consequently the resulting progress was not one of those sudden healings that occur in the lives of the hysterically afflicted; but it was a dogged, slow-moving, deter-mined process of mind over matter, of will over the fatalistic tendency to accept a physical condition as being hopeless.

The patient was a young man of fine physique, who had always been proud of his bodily development, his masculinity, and his ability to fend for himself and for his young wife and two children. In his mind, to be crippled or deformed in any way represented the tragedy of tragedies.

He had been carried into the hospital one day from the rock quarry with both arms broken, each one in two separate places. The unusual method employed in setting bones proved inadequate in his case and surgery was resorted to in the end.

The bones knitted splendidly, but there was the faintest overlapping of nerve lines, which left the boy's arms from the elbows down log-like and life-less. Apparently nothing could be done about it; but the surgeon dropped a hint that if the unfortunate could be made to concentrate the full force of his will on the problem and keep trying to move the dead fingers, he might eventually succeed in bringing about a realignment of the nerve carriers and thus regain the use of his arms.

The patient, however, had been completely over-come by the tragedy. All the interest he had ever had in life seemed to have left him when the full truth of his condition was finally forced upon him. Almost daily some of his relatives visited him. At first he could hardly bear the thought of seeing his wife and children. Unfortunately, through their strong efforts to pacify him, they succeeded in establishing in his mind a sort of dull acceptance, and he began to reconcile himself to a future of invalidism. Of course, so long as he remained in this attitude of mind, there was no use trying to reason with him about the necessity of making an effort. Every one about him did that to no avail. He would pretend to try, tire quickly, and slump back in his pillows.

While I watched these futile attempts being made to arouse an interest in him, I came to the conclusion that his case was to be absent of pandering sympathy.

This fellow had to be handled with brutal frankness and infinite patience, and infinite encouragement. To that task I dedicated myself.

I pictured to him with all the powers of description I could command, the horrors of an armless future, of his being a life-long object of charity, depending on others for every crust he ate, for every rag he wore. He was forced to grit his teeth to keep from screaming while I savagely mapped out the course his life must take. In the face of it he did exactly what I wanted him to do, he became desperate, he had been stirred to the foundation of his soul. At this juncture I said: "Remember, kid, it's up to you. If you want this sort of future you can have it. If you don't want it, you don't have to take it."

My last sentence kindled fires of hope in his eyes. He could not wait to begin the battle. I patted his shoulder in appreciation of his courage. "I'll explain how to go about it," I told him then.

And with this I told him about the creative principle that operated throughout the universe that could be contacted by love; that if his love for his arms was strong enough to make him try ceaselessly to move his fingers, the creative principle could be made to do his bidding.

His efforts were pathetically heroic. In order to make it less difficult, I advised him to direct his will into the right hand first. For three weeks I spent every spare minute I had at his bedside giving him encouragement. Sometimes he would think he felt his fingers move. And I would say, "You're right, they did move just a tremor." These lies were creative lies, because they created in him greater determination and greater effort.

As I watched one night my long vigil was rewarded.

His thumb moved. I grabbed him around the neck and shouted. I staggered from the room blind with gratitude.

I was never to have the satisfaction of seeing much further progress than that made, however, for about this time his relatives succeeded in getting him paroled because of the injury he had received while in prison. He was the only man to whom I've ever begrudged freedom. I believed then and I still believe that had I been given another month with him, his arms would have been restored. But during my remaining period in prison I heard of him from time to time. They had him in the care of many doctors who had tried in vain to help him. He had promised me on the day he left that he would keep trying our method. But many over-indulgent hands, I'm afraid, eager to do the work that his were made to do, broke down the desperate desire I had built up in him. At any rate, the last word I had of him proved him to be no better off than he was on the day he left prison.

*   *   *   *   *

A lways love causes something to be created. But always love must direct the creative principle toward constructive ends if such are the ends desired. I do not say this boy's friends and relatives consciously sought destruction for him. Indeed they did not. But the love they had for him was not the wise love that gives others the necessary stimulus and encouragement to help themselves.

The mother who loves her child so much that she relieves her child of self developing effort, is not loving constructively, and because she is not loving constructively a price will later be exacted of both her and the child. For always the creative principle creates that which it is directed to create. This is its nature.

And this is what it does. It is man's duty to use the creative principle toward constructive ends to the fullest extent of his capacity to do so. And this capacity is sometimes greater than man might at first realize. In other words, one never knows what one can do until one tries.

If every man would pause to question the course his desires were taking, and change that course if he found it to be destructive, this old world would soon notice a mighty falling off on the debit side of misery.

In this last particular I have saved a most unusual case through which to show how the creative principle, reversed, brought happiness to a man who for years had rolled himself about in a wheel-chair, grumbling at his fate, bored with the terrible monotony of his existence.

His physical handicap was of small importance compared to the sullen, brooding melancholia that made the contemplation of life far more terrible than contemplation of death. He had to be watched constantly in order to prevent him from carrying out and achieving what he had attempted on two or three occasions. A sufferer from insomnia, he would lie through the endless nights wide-eyed, cursing and grumbling; with the coming of morning he faced the day with the deadening horror of exhaustion, each moment passing with the slow pace of a century. All day long he would roll himself back and forth from his room to the clock at the far end of the corridor, note the time and then curse the hands that moved so slowly round the dial.

Being irritable and constantly cranky, he had no friends. In fact, he was one man who seemed unwilling to share his misery with others. To speak to him in a friendly tone was to court immediate rebuke, and only those unfamiliar with his scathing tongue ever invited it.

He had been a patient in the hospital for nearly a year when I began my duties there. I was promptly warned against him, told that no one would have anything to do with him. But this well-intentioned advice, instead of prejudicing me against the man, awakened within me a compassion so great that I found it difficult to contain it. I wanted to pour it out on him in a torrential flow of words. However, I held myself in check, bided my time, studied him minutely, and watched for him to show some sign of responsiveness. My reward came one day when I saw him watching the antics of a stray dog that had somehow slipped by the guard and found its way in to the prison yard. This display of interest struck me that he might be interested in a pet. I revealed my finding to the warden and got his permission to allow the man to have a small pet in his room.

I first thought of trying to secure a white mouse; but before I had a chance to make arrangements for one, a friend of mine found a young sparrow on the flag-stones of one of the cell buildings. The little fellow's right wing was broken. I brought it into the hospital and began to set the broken member. As I worked the patient rolled up in his chair and sat watching me silently. I turned to him and said, "I think I ought to wire the bones." And then I asked him to hold the bird while I went for the silver wire.

In a few minutes we were working together over our little cockney friend. With the operation completed, I hinted that I hated to turn the bird loose till it was well, but I didn't have time to look after it.

"I'll take care of it for you," he volunteered.

And how he took care of it! No bird ever got the

love and attention that he lavished on Molly, as he later named her. She thrived on his care. Her wing knitted and grew strong. He taught her many little tricks. She would ride about perched on his head; she would cling to his ear and chatter, while he chattered back. She would cling to his finger and take food from his tongue.

Then one day he grew pensive and told me he had decided to give Molly her freedom. I'll never forget that day. I went with him to the window and pushed the screen back for him. When Molly flew out, all that life held for him seemed to go with her. We watched her as she flew chattering here and there, lighting on this building and that, until finally we lost her and turned from the window. She remained away all day. But late in the afternoon I was awakened by his shout at my door. Jumping up I ran into his room. And there was Molly clinging to the outside of the screen, fussing and fluttering her wings in the utmost impatience with our stupidity and slowness in coming to her rescue.

Every day after that Molly was allowed to go out; but always about the same time in the afternoon she would reappear to be let in again. When the clock told him it was time to expect Molly home, he would roll himself to the window to welcome her.

Out of this incident I was able to establish other interests in this patient. He became an expert with needle and thread and made many beautiful things which he sold to visitors. A part of this money he set aside for charity purpose which he conducted among the hospital patients. Little things they needed that were not furnished by the prison he would buy and distribute. His name became a symbol of kindness throughout the prison. They called him a square guy, the highest compliment one convict can pay to another. And those he befriended during their stay in the hospital seldom forgot. Though he had no friends or relatives outside, on holidays, when boxes were allowed to be sent in, he was the recipient of more gifts than any one else in the prison. All of these gifts would come from his inmate friends; men fortunate enough to have friends and relatives outside to remember them.

The money he didn't use for charity was hoarded carefully until he had enough saved to purchase a set of books on commercial drafting. With these books he was busy preparing himself for a useful future when I was released. So completely occupied was he with this and his numerous other activities, he found it necessary to budget his time, allowing so much for this thing and so much for that. He has been given permission to use a bed lamp after the regular hour for retiring, and in this way he could carry on until midnight, at which time he would go to bed. Having trained himself to induce instant sleep, he would rest perfectly for six hours, at the end of which another busy day would begin.

How different his life was from those other days of dragging torment and those endless nights of sleeplessness. Then, each minute in the twenty-four hours meant just a link in an endless chain of monotony; now, each minute was a gem, too precious to be wasted in destructive thought and idleness.

It was a miracle in the realm of transformation; but it was an inevitable miracle. It could have been no other way. The moment he began to use the creative principle of life in the right direction, that moment he began to displace misery with happiness. This man confided many jewels of wisdom to me before my departure, but I've always held the following to be his richest bit of prison philosophy.

"Don't seek peace," he told me, *"but conflict. By conflict we grow, and growth is just another name for happiness."*

CHAPTER 8
Love Can Open
Prison Doors of Steel

*Great men are they who see that spiritual is stronger
than any material force, that thoughts rule the world.*

—Emerson.

All men accept the idea that love and thought are
synonymous, that the former is the first expression of the latter, and that the combination of the
intellectual and emotional form a unity inseparable
one from the other, and that this unity, acting upon
creative principle, constitutes the strongest creative
force in the world.

All men admit that thought-force is capable of
performing miracles, of constantly changing the face
of things, of brushing aside the impossible, and out of
the impossible of yesterday establishing the common-
place of today. Men will agree to the truism that the
possible accomplishments of thought are limitless;
but when you say that thought can open the doors of
a modern prison, unsupported by collusion or
political influence, men will shake their heads, thus
indicating their Missourian disposition to be shown.

On an evening in 1924 I sat in a cell alone on the
receiving gallery of the prison mentioned throughout
this book. My outlook was as black and hopeless as
any man's outlook could possibly be. That morning I
had been up before the board of paroles, and the

chairman of the board, who had done the talking, had been in no mood to spare my sensibilities.

Only a very short while before I faced the same body of men, and I had made them the usual run of glowing promises. "Yes, gentlemen," I had said on that occasion, "when I go out this time I intend to make good. I've learned my lesson. This jolt has taught me that crime doesn't pay. I'm done with it forever. Me for the straight and narrow from now on."

"Well, this has been your second offence in this prison," the chairman had replied. "Yet your prison record has been fairly good. We've decided to give you another chance. But if you fail, if you come back again you may expect no consideration at our hands."

And I had gone out a few mornings later. The man who signed my parole and who had worked for my release because of his friendship for my father, received me in a spirit of paternal trust and confidence. And that very night I took up again where I had left off when the prison door had cut short my criminal career. I had no intention of trying to make good. I had merely repeated my old meaningless promises in exchange for official favors. So when I sat before the parole board on this morning I wore the brand of an habitual criminal. The chairman said to me:

"You've betrayed the trust we reposed in you. You were told what to expect if you did that. Now what have you to say for yourself?"

I had nothing to say, of course. What could I say? I had reached the end of my purring promises. I was at the end of my old reliable resources. I could say nothing but face the music and pay the fiddler.

"You've made your own bed," the chairman went

on ruthlessly, "and you've made it out of sand-burrs. It's going to be pretty tough to lie in. But you're going to lie in it this time. Your sentence calls for from one to twenty years. I wish we had power to make it life. You've forfeited every right to our sympathy. We cannot inflict more than the maximum sentence upon you, but we can inflict that, and you shall be made to serve every minute of that twenty years, which will amount to eleven years and three months under the 'good time law,' without ever again having an opportunity to appear before this board for consideration of parole matters."

My rating was not only that of an habitual criminal. My criminological rating had me listed as abnormal, criminally insane, incurably anti-social. I was hopelessly beyond the influence of reformation. The warden told me no power on earth save a miracle could ever shorten my sentence one minute.

And yet I sat before that same board five years later and listened to them talk to me in the friendliest tones. And again, a year later, I appeared before them again and received their assurance that I was deserving of another chance. They gave me that chance and I went out five years in advance of the time set for my release. Nor did I use any political or other influence whatever. Indeed, I had only one or two letters of recommendation on file in my behalf, and these were from persons who had no prestige or influential power with the state administration.

*   *   *   *   *

On that night in 1924 as I sat in my cell on the receiving gallery, my thoughts were fog-bound. I had been able to face short terms with a certain degree of equipoise for I could see through to the end; but now there was no end. Already dissipation had stamped me with premature old age. After eleven

years and three months I would be fit for nothing, save
to join the pathetic ranks of old broken-down prison
lags who, after making their weary rounds of the
various prisons, usually wound up by appearing voluntarily at some prison gate begging for admittance,
pleading for the privilege of entering and ending their
miserable days in the only sort of home they had ever
known.

Yes, by that time, my nerve would be completely
gone. I would not have enough left to commit another
crime in order to break back into prison. I would
come doddering back, burned out and shriveled up,
whining and begging for a home and finally a hole in
the prison grave-yard. I could see that sort of end; I
could see no other.

It was to be eleven years and three months on the
calendar; in the terms of emotion it would be a
thousand years. I hated myself that evening as no
man has ever hated. One does not know hate who has
only hated the conditions in which he lives; the emotion of hate that reaches no farther than to God, to
decency, to fairness, to other men, is not hate in its
blackest and bitterest sense. One must hate one's self,
wholly, completely, utterly, really to know what hate
means. And that is the way I hated on this dreary,
futureless evening.

I could see but one way out. A safety razor blade
would twist me out of my misery. But a better way
would be to die with the guns of the guards roaring in
my ears.

At least if I was rubbed out in an effort to escape I
would have made that one effort. The chances were
one in a thousand perhaps, for success. But, there was
still that one chance. It would be better to gamble
everything on it, than to go out the cowardly way.

As I was trying to choose between these two extremes, I hadn't known that self destruction actually was a cowardly way to avoid a bad situation. The prisoner in charge of the gallery brought this fact home to me. I told him in answer to his comment, "Looks kinda tough for you this trip," that if it got too tough I knew how to remedy the situation.

He cackled mirthlessly, "You won't be the first weakling to take that way out."

"It takes nerve to wind up your own ball of yarn," was my reply.

He cackled again. "No, you're wrong, it takes nerve to face the jolt you're facing—more nerve than you've got, old man. It's easier to hand in your checks."

I hadn't thought of self destruction in that light. Obviously he was right. Under the circumstances, it required little courage to face death; but to face the lingering torment of this living death, eleven years and three months of it—to face that took real courage.

It was courage, thank God, that challenged me to combat. I would not advertise to the whole prison that I was too much of a weakling to pay the piper. Nor would I knuckle down and become the docile, broken-spirited lamb. I would face the music, but I would face it as a rebel, a firebrand, a prison revolutionist.

Naturally, in this attitude of violence, I did nothing but injure myself. It was the same attitude I carried with me into the dungeon some three years later— and left there, never again to be resurrected.

*   *   *   *   *

That I could use the love medium to gain my freedom never occurred to me of my own accord. After I had discovered that medium and had began to apply it to my life and the lives of those around me, I was so thoroughly in harmony with my environment that time, place and conditions meant nothing. The days and nights came and went with a smoothness and velocity that was simply astounding. I seldom could tell any one the day of the week, and the date of the month was a thing I rarely ever knew. Once I was asked the day of the week. I didn't know. Then I was asked the date of the month, and I didn't know that either.

"Well, do you know what year it is?" asked my questioner. And studying some time I was able to answer that one. But my questioner promptly informed me that I was a year behind time.

So one day when a fellow, and he an official, asked why I didn't try to get my case up and get out, I was forced to admit that it had been a long time since I had thought of my freedom. I did think of it after that, however, although not in a way to disturb my peace of mind. I had reached the point where, like my old cell-mate, I didn't care where I was on earth, so long as I could carry on my experiments for the improvement of myself and others. *The idea of gaining my freedom now held out its reward, not in the freedom itself, but in the proof or demonstration that it could be gained by the application of love and thought to creative principle.*

When I made up my mind to try it I bumped into a string of questioning qualms. Always before I had used the principle for service to others or for the purpose of furthering my own spiritual and mental interests. To use it now merely to gain my freedom left a selfish tang in my soul that I drew back from in a sort of moral recoil. Even though Dad assured me that my qualms were unwarranted, the feeling continued to persist.

In meditation I sought assurance which didn't come immediately. The reason: I was shutting myself from the reservoir of intuitive knowledge by squeezing the channel with strain. I learned that when you seek the super consciousness for knowledge about a particular thing, you usually wind up disappointed with knowledge about nothing. These are most unsatisfying meditations.

My meditations before had been all-embracing. I sought meditation for the sheer joy of entering that far-flung realm of super joy. And consequently, having no human desire to hinder bodily relaxation or to prevent the gradual slowing down process of the heart and lungs to the state of pulselessness and breathlessness, I had been able to contact general wisdom almost at a moment's notice. But with a particular desire in my mind, I could neither relax nor receive, because the nature of the desire was always there, and nothing else could get through or around it.

However, as it later panned out, these futile attempts did impress themselves upon my subconscious mind, and the subconscious mind, in turn, took its directions and passed them on to me.

These directions were specific, but not understandable as applying to my problem. I got them in the form of a dream during subconscious meditation. I did not at first act upon them, because they seemed to have no connection with the one thing I wanted to know: "Would I now be justified in using the creative principle against others in order to influence them to grant me a favor I had come to consider purely selfish?"

Finally one evening, during a desireless meditation, I received the information that there was no such thing as selfishness. There was a *misuse* of supply and a *right* use of supply.

And with this, of course, I realized that my freedom rightly used would conform to life's purpose of spiritual growth, just the same as my imprisonment rightly used had done. We were punished not for our right uses of law, but for our misuses of law.

*   *   *   *   *

The directions I received had to do with the transmission of telepathic thought over a distance of many miles. The object of this thought-transmission was the chairman of the parole-board.

It entailed my having to learn something of this man's habits. Which I did, working through a friend of mine in the prison record clerk's office, and he in turn working through the private secretary of the chairman. I learned a great deal about the home the chairman occupied, its location. I learned that he usually retired at ten-thirty each night that business or pleasure did not prevent. Also, that for about two hours before retiring he sat alone in his library with his books. I learned many details about this library, its general appointments, its shape and location in the house, the reading lamp and the chair where he sat.

With all this information in my hands I was ready to begin *the biggest experiment I had yet undertaken, that of impressing my personality upon the mind of a man across a vast distance of space.* I had achieved the same thing many times at close range, and I had no doubt but that the same thing could be accomplished at long range. And I might add that this very faith was a great aid to that end.

What I did therefore was to visualize the chairman in his favorite chair in his library. I did this every night so as not to miss him on the nights he actually occupied this place. I surrounded him with an imaginary atmosphere of peace, contentment, comfort, receptiveness. I thought of him in terms of love, of Christliness. I talked to him with my thoughts, wishing him well. Night after night, in this imaginary manner, I hovered round. For several months I kept faithfully and patiently at the experiment, not once allowing myself to become discouraged in the face of the fact that nothing seemed to happen. Indeed, as the effort was extended, it seemed to become almost effortless. In time it grew into a pleasant endeavor. I grew to feel an exuberant joy in paying this man my nightly visit, and I also came to feel that he was finding his library period more and more pleasurable.

Eventually there was added to my directions another piece of business that apparently had no connection whatever to the business at hand, but was so urgent that I was forced to get in touch with Dad Trueblood, who of course had been informed of my experiment from the first.

I was given an urge to write an essay on a certain topic and to submit it to the editor of a certain welfare magazine. At this time the rules of the prison had not yet been lowered to that place where prisoners were allowed to write for publication. This restriction, however, was lifted soon after the event just described.

Dad's advice was prompt and to the point.

"Write the essay and send it," he said.

"But the warden won't stand for that," I told him. "Besides, what do I know about writing?"

"In this case you may find out you don't need to know anything about it after you get started. If the urge is genuine, the thing will write itself. Anyway it's up to you to go ahead."

"Well," I told him, "I don't know what it's all about, but I'm game to try anything once."

I don't know whether the essay was good or not.

Dad said it was. The warden said it was. The chairman of the board said it was. The point is, it was because of it that I was called that second time before the parole-board, five years after my first appearance before that body, at which time I had been told I would never be called there again for consideration of parole matters. As a matter of fact I wasn't called there for the consideration of parole matters. But of that later.

After I had finished the essay I carried it to the warden and asked him if I could send it to the magazine indicated. His answer was a flat refusal. But he read the essay. When he had finished, he looked at me with surprise.

"Did you write this?" he wanted to know.

I admitted the fact.

"Well, it's good," he said, "and I'm going to put it in the hands of the chairman of the board." As I rose to leave he added: "You've been making a mighty good record lately. Keep it up."

When the parole board held its next session at the prison I was called before it. My essay was lying on the table in front of the chairman when I entered. I was greeted cordially and told to sit down. The chairman informed me that I was not there because they had decided to reopen my case. He picked up the essay and asked me if I had written it.

"Yes, sir," I replied. "Or rather it was written for me. My work was merely stenographic."

He laughed. "Well, whoever wrote it," he said, "has expressed sentiments that make for good citizen-ship."

There was more said, of course, and while I have not given the verbatim account of the conversation, because I do not remember the precise words, I have employed dialogue to express the general trend of the thought. So it has been throughout the writing of this book wherever conversation has been employed. Where I have been able to record conversation verbatim, I've done so; where I haven't, due to a lack of memory, I've tried to copy the actual as nearly as I could.

Following this incident, I no longer pursued my experimentation along the telepathic line. I knew that the chairman of the board now had me in mind and I knew that my prison conduct was being closely watched at the chairman's request.

I conducted myself as before. I went ahead with my work and proceeded to forget all about my freedom. When an opportunity arose whereby I could use the creative principle constructively against the problems of my fellows, I did so. A year thus passed. Then I was called before the board again. This time to receive my freedom.

$$* \quad * \quad * \quad * \quad *$$

The subject of thought transference is today under the fire of controversy. I have neither desire nor intention of presenting this experience as a contribution to telepathic lore. The argument for or against has no appeal for me whatever. There may not be such a possibility as transferring thought although my belief is on the positive side. The weight of my evidence is found in the results obtained through my experiments.

In this chapter I have described as nearly as I was able, the exact method used to gain my freedom, to open the door of my prison. That this method was responsible for the opening of that door, I sincerely believe to be true. The reader may believe otherwise. That is a privilege I deny no one. But I might say in addition, that apart from my description of what occurred, there is some documentary evidence. The record of this prison will show that I entered there in the year previously mentioned; that my sentence was set at eleven years and three months; and that without political or other influences of any kind, I was released from there five years in advance of the time fixed by law.

My experience in the prison hospital was rich with evidence that thought was easily transferred from one mind to another. In one of the many cases of hysterically induced diseases, I used the telepathic method exclusively.

The boy was a patient in the tubercular ward. A few months before he had been in the best of health. Then one day he picked up a handkerchief near the hospital, took it to his cell, washed it and began to use it. A day or two later a friend seeing him with an outside store-bought handkerchief, asked him where he got it, and the boy told him.

"Why you big fool," said the friend. "I'll bet one of them T.B.'s over there threw it out of the window. They're always doing things like that. They want other people to catch the T.B."

The boy became panicky and began to brood constantly on what his friend had told him. His appetite began to fade away. He lost weight and lived in daily and nightly dread of the terrifying disease. Then he caught a slight cold and developed a cough. He was sure he had taken tuberculosis. He came on the sick-call to the hospital and voiced his fears to the doctor. He was put in a room while an examination was made. He carried no temperature; a sputum test revealed the presence of no germs. But he could not be convinced, and a few weeks later when another test was made, he was running a temperature and the sputum revealed germs.

In the tuberculosis ward I tried every way I could think of to rid his mind of this morbid disease-thought. But the thought was so deeply grooved in his subconscious mind that no amount of conscious suggestion could counter-groove it.

I decided to try telepathy on him while he slept. I knew of course that these patients were super-sensitive and super receptive to thought force during their waking hours. But I had never tried to influence one of them while he slept.

At night time in the ward, after nine o'clock, all the lights were turned off, except one red one in the middle of the room. Thus I could slip in quietly, make my way through the semi-darkness, and thus reach his bed-side without disturbing his slumber. Crouching directly behind the head of his bed, I mentally called his name, concentrating the full force of my faculties upon its clear deliberate and sonorous enunciation.

At first I got no visible response. Duties inter-vening, I was compelled to conduct my experiment at short intervals throughout that first night. The following night also evinced nothing in the way of reward for my efforts. But about three o'clock in the morning of the third night, he began to manifest a sense of restlessness during the period I slowly pronounced his name. When my thoughts of him were withdrawn, he would immediately become quiet and begin again to breathe evenly.

Of course, I was elated. To me these incidents were not the accidental disturbances of dream states. I was firmly convinced that he was being influenced, not by internal forces, but by a force of thought exuded from my own mind. However, before I accepted this conviction, I saw the same thing demonstrated repeatedly in more than a hundred precise experiments.

The last one of its kind conducted, that is, in which his response was merely a nervous display, happened in the presence of the night-warder of the hospital and the night-captain of the guard. More than a dozen times they witnessed his disturbance while I called to him. And then when I would raise my hand, indicating to them that I was going to withdraw my influence, they saw the tension leave him while he began his quiet even process of breathing once more.

The next experiment brought forth in addition to his physical reaction, a verbal response. Yet I refused to accept this as anything genuinely connected with the experiment until he had repeated it numerous times during the period of my operations. He at no time spoke over the one word while the experiment was going on. That one word was mother. It was garbled somewhat, as most words spoken in dreams. But the thing that was striking about it was that the inflection was always the same. It was as though his mother appeared to him in a dream and as though he had been expecting her to come. Now the boy's mother was dead; but it was obvious the memory of her still influenced his sub-conscious life.

At this point I made an assumption that, naturally I had no way of proving whether or not it was working out as I assumed it to be working out. But when he would speak the word mother, I would assume that her personality and influence were with him in a dream, and I endeavored to make her say the things I wanted her to say. In other words, while her personality was visible to him in his dream, I assumed that I was she and I spoke to him with my thoughts in terms of his health, seeking always, through telepathic suggestion, to counteract the effect of disease-thought held in his sub-consciousness, and to replace the disease thought with the thought of health.

This treatment, together with a carefully planned tissue-building diet, I am certain was responsible for this patient's final and complete recovery from the disease that had taken him very close to death. I am aware that this incident can prove nothing on behalf of the believers of thought-transference. But then the motive for my experiment was not to seek proof for or against a theory. My first interest was in the welfare of my patient, and my gratitude came when I was able to witness his steady but certain progress toward recovery. My big thrill of joy arrived on the day the doctor dismissed him from the hospital with a high rating of health.

*   *   *   *   *

Love and the creative principle. These words mean absolutely nothing. But to take what they symbolize and incorporate it into the daily livingness of one's life, means that that *one has the key that will unlock all the doors that limit one, in proportion as one's capacity increases for receiving and using creative power through the medium of love.*

Jesus could use creative power greatly, because He loved greatly. When one's sense of brotherly love is strong enough to die for the future betterment of one's fellowmen, such a one becomes a magnificent user of creative power and leaves a heritage the like of which has kept and will continue to keep the human family in existence and growing toward its goal of spiritual perfection.

What I have been able to achieve with creative power is small when compared to what I should like to achieve. In the minds of my readers, my achievement may not seem great; but to me it is monumental. I have no doubt, that without this key my prison door would still be locked against me, had I not died long ago from the toxic poisons generated in my system by hate and the philosophy of negation.

For this key I am humbly and enormously grateful.

THE END

Made in the USA
Columbia, SC
02 April 2024

33943370R00089